TROILUS AND CRISEYDE

A Critical Study

CHAUCER'S TROILUS AND CRISEYDE

A Critical Study

Ian Bishop

University of Bristol

Published by the University of Bristol

ISBN 0 906515 84 X

Designed and produced by the
University of Bristol Information Office
Printed by the University of Bristol Printing Unit

Contents

Preface

The intention of this monograph on *Troilus and Criseyde* is to offer a balanced, critical reading of the poem as a whole, founded upon a close study of the way in which the poetic language functions in its narrative context. In order to keep Chaucer's poem continuously in the foreground of this brief study, I have, as far as possible, avoided polemic. Some indications of the ways in which my reading of the poem differs from those of other commentators may be found in the notes; but the main function of those notes is to indicate some part of my debt to the labours and insights of earlier scholars and critics. M. Salu (ed.), *Essays on Troilus and Criseyde* (D. S. Brewer Ltd., 1979) was published too recently for me to be able to make use of it in the present study.

It is a pleasure to acknowledge particular debts of gratitude to various friends and colleagues. Above all, I am indebted to John Burrow who, after reading the typescript of this study, offered valuable criticisms from which I have tried to profit; and to Myra Stokes who very kindly undertook to correct the proofs. I am also grateful to the University of Bristol Publications Committee for undertaking the publication of the book; to the university's Information Officer and to the staff of the Printing Office for much help and advice; to the. Trustees of the Winston Churchill Birthday Foundation for a grant to cover expenses incurred in preparing this book for publication. Mrs. Anne Merriman typed my manuscript; my wife gave practical help of various kinds. Finally, I must express my gratitude to several generations of undergraduates at the University of Bristol for the stimulus of discussion and argument about Chaucer's poem. In particular, I would thank them for enabling me to challenge – through *experience* rather than *auctoritee* – C. S. Lewis's assertion concerning Criseyde (*The Allegory of Love,* p. 182) that 'as more and more women take up the study of English Literature she is likely to find ever less mercy'.

Ian Bishop
Bristol, 1980

List of Abbreviations

CR	–	*The Chaucer Review*
CT	–	*The Canterbury Tales*
E & S	–	*Essays & Studies by Members of the English Association*
EETS	–	*Early English Texts Society*
ELH	–	*English Literary History*
GGK	–	*Sir Gawain & the Green Knight*
HoF	–	*The House of Fame*
JEGP	–	*Journal of English and Germanic Philology*
LGW	–	*The Legend of Good Women*
MLQ	–	*Modern Language Quarterly*
N & Q	–	*Notes & Queries*
PoF	–	*The Parlement of Foules*
PMLA	–	*Publications of the Modern Language Association (of America)*
RES	–	*Review of English Studies*
SP	–	*Studies in Philology*

PART ONE:
THE ACTORS

Chapter One
The Lovers and their Histories

When, in his uncompromising Retractions, the repentant Chaucer made his last recorded reference to the longest of his completed narrative poems, he remembered it as 'the book of Troilus' (*CT*. X. 1083—86). Such a title may seem appropriate enough for a work that begins by purporting:

> The double sorwe of Troilus to tellen,
> That was the kyng Priamus sone of Troye,
> In lovynge how his aventures fellen
> Fro wo to wele, and after out of joie.[1]

— and, having accordingly described the curve of the hero's life, even proceeds to a tangential account of the flight of his soul to the Ogdoad. On the other hand, it is by the heroine's infamous name that he causes Alceste to recall the poem, more in sorrow than in anger, in *The Legend of Good Women* (F. 441; G. 451).

The way in which the opening lines allow a double portion of sorrow (and, consequently, of sympathy) to the hero, and refer to his love without mentioning its object, may be taken as either a slighting of the heroine or else an attempt to shield her. For it seems that the poet's reticence about her in this opening sentence is a calculated silence. This is suggested by the way in which the eight stanzas that constitute the poem's prologue are so arranged that they conclude with a recapitulation of that sentence. But it is a *reprise* with a difference:

> For now wol I gon streyght to my matere,
> In which ye may the double sorwes here
> Of Troilus in lovynge of Criseyde,
> And how that she forsook hym or she deyde.
>
> (I. 53—56)

He goes 'streyght to [the] matere', not only because he here broaches his narrative, but also because he at last brings himself to associate his hero with the woman whose betrayal of him constitutes the fable's *raison d'être*. In doing so he pronounces upon her the most downright condemnation she is to receive from him. Just as we may find some of the narrator's comments in Book V, after her yielding to Diomede, a little too indulgent, so the bald statement here of her future conduct may strike us as too unkind in its abruptness. Yet Chaucer can afford to make the later extenuating gestures only because he has already stated the worst that can be said about her. Such is his characteristic way of representing the truth about a character.

Chaucer's combination of reluctance and abruptness in mentioning his heroine may be a reaction to his *auctoures* and what they had made of her. He writes like one who is embarrassed by the fact that, in order to relate the 'unsely aventure' of the 'worthy' Troilus, it is necessary to mention Criseyde at all and so stir up again the muddy waters in which her 'name' is drowned. But the attentive reader will have noticed that Chaucer has already introduced a hint that suggests he is capable of representing fairly the conduct of both parties to the relationship. In the prologue he had urged his audience to pray for various categories of lovers, including 'hem that falsly ben apeired / Thorugh wikked tonges, be it he or she' (I. 38—39). The parenthesis, 'be it he or she', is, in its context in the middle of the Prologue, less obtrusive than the famous address at the beginning of the Epilogue to 'yonge, fresshe folkes, he or she' (V. 1835) — where Chaucer pointedly departs from Boccaccio's exclusive address to young men whom he warns of the fickleness of many young women.[2] But, though it is less conspicuous, it is hardly less significant.

As with several of the poet's apparently simple statements of intent, his initial description of his 'matere' cannot be taken as a straightforward or adequate synopsis of what is to follow. An objective 'advertisement' of the 'argument' of the poem that Chaucer wrote would hardly have omitted the following facts:

> A beautiful young widow, left in Troy by her father when he deserted to the besieging Greeks, is wooed in secret by a Trojan prince who eventually wins her with the help of her uncle, Pandare. Later she exchanges Troilus for an inferior lover; but only after she has herself been exchanged, as a political pawn, from one belligerent power to the other.

When Criseyde is thus seen as abandoned by her father, manipulated by her uncle and traded by the politicians before she exchanges Troilus for Diomede, she may even appear as one more sinned against than sinning. The treacherousness of her environment is further emphasised by the fact that the poem's historical narrative is framed by acts of treason: not only is it preceded by Calchas's desertion, but it is followed by the treachery of Antenor (cf. IV. 197—203) — the very man for whom she was so dishonourably exchanged by the Trojan 'parlement'. Troilus's 'trouthe' shines out like bright metal upon this sullen ground. Nevertheless, even his conduct is not wholly unalloyed with treacherous inclinations. None of the 'loveres', to whom the poem is addressed, would criticise him for the way in which he is prepared (in Book IV) to abandon family, friends and his native land at the hour of their greatest need so that he might elope with Criseyde — especially when they recalled the Trojan parliament's dishonourable treatment of his beloved.

But they might feel uneasy at his connivance, however reluctant, at Pandarus's petty deceptions of his niece. More positively discreditable is the occasion when, in order to dispel Pandarus's scruples about the office he has undertaken on his behalf, he makes himself into his friend's similitude by offering to procure for him any of his royal sisters — whether 'Polixene, / Cassandre, Eleyne, or any of the frape' (III. 409–10). Though the widespread pattern of treachery in the world of Chaucer's poem cannot excuse Criseyde's betrayal of her lover, it nevertheless helps to explain the fact that, where Boccaccio concludes his narrative with a specific condemnation of the heroine's behaviour, Chaucer substitutes a general condemnation of 'false worldes brotelnesse' (V. 1832).

The presence of this *moralitee*, no less than the references to the power of Fortune — 'traitour comune' (IV. 5) — over sublunary affairs, appears to have encouraged some modern critics to disregard some of the more interesting aspects of Chaucer's representation of the behaviour of a 'false' heroine. For example, one influential critic, after making some shrewd comments on her role in the earlier books, concludes that, when it comes to the account of her treachery, she must be regarded not so much as a 'psychological entity' as a symbol of secular life. He writes:

> The meaning of the poem does not hinge on so *fortuitous* a fact as Troilus's placing his faith in the wrong woman or in a bad woman, but in the fact that he places his faith in a *thing* which can reflect back to him the image of that faith and yet be incapable of sustaining it.[3]

This certainly states an important truth about Troilus's attitude towards her. But her function is more organic than that of a mirror: it is often that of an eye through which the reader obtains a partial view of the action. At times her vision is remarkably penetrating; at others it sees merely what it is conditioned to see or what it chooses to see, and is often blind to phenomena which the narrative clearly shows to be present — as she herself admits when she laments that she always lacked one of Prudence's 'eyen thre' (V. 744–49).

Criseyde, hardly less than Troilus, is one of the principal centres of consciousness in the narrative and is viewed from the inside as well as from without. The effect upon Chaucer's creative imagination of the need to present a 'false' heroine is to cause him to represent the lovers' relationship, as it were, contrapuntally rather than merely harmonically; this makes for a much more subtle style of narration. The narrative brings together in the most searching of human relationships two very different personalities, of diverse origins and dissimilar destinies, who are endowed with contrasted modes of consciousness. Whether or not they are presented as consistent 'psychological entities', they are certainly heard as distinctive voices and make their independent contributions to a continually shifting dialectic.

Their different sensibilities may be seen in their separate reactions to the historical process that envelops them: both exhibit an uneasy awareness of being actors in a narrative composed by someone else; but each has different opinions about its author's identity. The first occasion when Criseyde shows herself to be aware of being circumscribed in this way occurs in the first scene of Book II when Pandarus has at last revealed the true purpose of his visit. She exclaims resentfully and bitterly:

> 'What! Is this al the joye and al the feste?
> Is this youre reed? is this my blisful cas?
> Is this the verray mede of youre byheste?
> Is al this peynted proces seyd, allas!
> Right for this fyn? ...'
>
> (II. 421–25)

Her speech comprises an anthology of the choicest phrases from Pandarus's devious prolegomena to his announcement of Troilus's love; but it is an anthology from which the blooms have been plucked, leaving only the briers with which she proceeds to scratch her uncle's face. She is apprehensive of the way in which the 'peynted proces' of her uncle's insidious diplomacy threatens to shape her life into what Chaucer elsewhere calls 'a proces or a tale', into a romantic idyll, in which she is cast to play the part of heroine, but of which she is not herself the author. Her resistance to the 'fyn' towards which she is being propelled begins to falter when she reflects upon the aimlessness of her widowed life: 'to what fyn live I thus?' (II. 757). But this impulse is partly checked by the contrary query, 'To what fyn is swich love' (II. 794), and she does not finally surrender to her lover until she reaches a point where she can believe that she has herself had a major hand in the composition of the script. She tells Troilus that she had anticipated this surrender in her imagination long before she permitted it to occur in practice:

> 'Ne hadde I or now, my swete herte deere,
> Ben yolde, iwys, I were now nat here.'
>
> (III. 1210–11)

It may seem to the observer, however, that she has done little more than decelerate the 'proces' set in motion by Pandarus. In Book IV she makes a gesture of independence by rejecting Troilus's plan for elopement in favour of a rather devious 'proces' of her own. But, in effect, she thereby merely complies with the politicians' designs for her and discovers too late that what she thought to be her own invention has led her into a snare (V. 748). It ultimately renders her vulnerable to the designs of a far less considerate manipulator than her uncle.

Troilus likewise considers himself to be encompassed by a 'proces' when, in Book V, he is wondering, with diminishing hope, whether his lady will ever return from the enemy camp. But the author of the 'proces' that appears to be shaping his life into a 'tragedye' is no mere mortal:

> Then thoughte he thus: 'O blisful lord Cupide,
> Whan I the *proces* have in my memorie,
> How thow me hast werreyed on every syde,
> *Men myghte a book make of it lik a storie.*
> What nede is the to seke on me victorie,
> Syn I am thyn, and holly at thi wille?
> What joie hastow thyn owen folk to spille?
>
> 'Wel hastow, lord, ywroke on me thyn ire,
> Thow myghty god, and dredful for to greve.
> Now mercy, lord; thow woost wel I desire
> Thi grace moost of alle lustes leeve.
> And lyve and dye I wol in thy byleve;
> For which I naxe in guerdoun but a bone,
> That thow Criseyde ayein me sende sone ...
>
> 'Now, blisful lord, so cruel thow ne be
> Unto the blood of Troie, I preye the,
> As Juno was unto the blood Thebane,
> For which the folk of Thebes caughte hire bane.'
> (V. 582–602)

The 'proces', of which Troilus has at last become aware, has been presented by the poet as the inevitable nemesis for the prince's initial, hubristic scorn of Cupid and his votaries as 'Seynt Idyot, lord of thise foles alle' (I. 910). The athletic prince taunted the lovers in his retinue with being huntsmen engaged in the futile pursuit of an elusive quarry:

> 'And which a labour folk han in wynnynge
> Of love, and in the kepyng which doutaunces;
> And whan youre preye is lost, wo and penaunces.'
> (I. 199–201)

Cupid persecutes his blasphemer by making him run this very course himself: he is made to suffer in turn each of the symptoms described in these lines. The repentant and enamoured Troilus of Book I is deceived into thinking that he has already endured the full measure of 'wo and penaunces'. When Pandarus hears that Troilus is in love he cheerfully forecasts that his converted friend will become a pillar of love's religion (I. 1000–01). Up to the end of Book III there seems much to be cheerful about as Troilus enters into love's Heaven on Earth. But, although he begins as a pillar of love's church, he ends by being tied to the stake as love's martyr. In the ensuing 'tragedye' he learns that his sufferings in Book I comprised merely the 'labour folk han in wynnynge

/ Of love'. In Book IV he experiences 'in the kepying which doutaunces' and not until Book V does he drink the full potion of 'wo and penaunces' that Cupid has prescribed for his victim. Troilus has to learn by experience the proper respect for Cupid which the narrator of *The Parlement of Foules,* who claims no direct knowledge of love, has learnt from the 'authority' of books:

> For al be that I knowe nat Love in dede,
> Ne wot how that he quiteth folk hire hyre,
> Yit happeth me ful ofte in bokes reede
> Of his myrakles and his crewel yre.
> Ther rede I wel he wol be lord and syre;
> I dar nat seyn, his strokes been so sore,
> But 'God save swich a lord!' — I can na moore.
>
> (8—14)

But, then, one of the books he had read contained the story of Troilus (cf. 291).

It is characteristic of Troilus to find himself the victim of daemonic principalities and powers: Cupid here and Fortune elsewhere. It is equally characteristic of Criseyde (the sceptical daughter of a treacherous priest) that she should tend to believe herself practised against by nothing more than the deceitful stratagems of men. Even her profound outburst against 'fals felicitee' (III. 813—36) is occasioned by her belief that Troilus has become jealous of her on account of 'Horaste'. In keeping with this difference of outlook is the fact that when Troilus at last has Criseyde naked in his arms his first reaction is to address a hymn of thanksgiving to Love, giving him the honorific title of 'Charity', and not forgetting to mention in due order his mother 'Citherea the swete' (alternatively, 'Venus ... the wel-willy planete') and Hymen (III. 1247—75). But when Criseyde surrenders wholly to her lover, she permits no gods to come between them. Troilus is all-sufficient to her: 'Welcome! my knyght, my pees, my suffisaunce' (III. 1309). Similarly, it is appropriate that Chaucer should follow his hero — the idealist who is endowed with such a sensitive consciousness of the operation of supernatural powers — to the point where, after death, he catches a glimpse of eternal truth, the power 'Uncircumscript, and al maist circumscrive'. Criseyde, on the other hand, is left where she is still circumscribed by secular life, as she makes her pathetic resolution of eternal stability: 'To Diomede algate I wol be trewe' (V. 1071).

There is, however, a sense in which Chaucer does not leave her there. After she has decided to let herself be taken to the Greek camp, she protests to Troilus that, if ever she should prove false to him, may Juno

> 'As wood as Athamante do me dwelle
> Eternelich in Stix, the put of helle.'
>
> (IV. 1539—40)

Chaucer makes no excursion to the inferno, corresponding to his ascent to the Ogdoad, to see whether her shade has its abode there. Nevertheless, an even more shadowy part of her does survive to endure its punishment in the after-life. She foresees that 'thise bokes' will preserve her 'name' to be rolled upon the tongues of generations of detractors — especially women (V. 1058—64). The extension of Criseyde's consciousness to include an accurate prediction of her posthumous reputation (up to Chaucer's time) is a more subtle punishment than the prostitution and the leprosy that Henryson causes to be visited upon her. Its aptness will become apparent if we consider the importance that Chaucer causes her to attach to her 'name' and the way in which her concern for it supplied the motive for her most crucial decision in the 'tragedye'.

From the moment near the beginning of the narrative, when we are assured that 'wel men of hir tolde' (I. 131), we have never been allowed to overlook her regard for her 'honeste'. Pandarus, in order to discover who is the object of Troilus's love, has physically to shake his friend, exclaiming: 'thef, thow shalt hyre name telle' (I. 870). As soon as the lover discloses it, Chaucer plays with the word *name,* in its literal and figurative senses, throughout the whole of a stanza:

> And whan that Pandare herde hire *name nevene,*
> Lord, he was glad, and seyde: 'frende so deere,
> Now fare aright, for Joves *name* in hevene,
> Love hath byset the wel; be of good cheere,
> For *of good name,* wisdom, and manere
> She hath ynough, and ek of gentilesse;
> If she be fayre, thow woost thy self, I gesse.'
> (I. 876—92)

Later in the same speech Pandarus returns to the point:

> 'Requere nat that is ayeyns hyre name!'   (I. 902)

The word-play seems to imply that, for Criseyde, reputation, her *simulacrum* that she presents to the world, is almost indistinguishable from her essential identity. This is understandable in one whose beauty makes her seem like 'an hevenyssh perfit creature'; and there are urgent circumstantial reasons why she, as a public traitor's daughter, should be anxious about preserving the untarnished sheen of her social 'image' — to employ the vogue word of our decade. But, as the narrative develops, she seems to cultivate an almost narcissistic regard for this flattering and comforting reflection. In Book III Pandarus, when urging secrecy upon Troilus, concludes a stanza by beseeching him: 'Syn thow art wys, so save alwey hire name'; and begins the next:

> 'For wel thow woost, the name as yit of hire
> Among the peple, as who seyth, halwed is ...'
> (III. 267—68)

Her name is held by the people as a thing enskied and sainted, only 'in a manner of speaking' ('as who seyth'). But her behaviour in Book IV suggests that she regards it *in fact* as her most sacred possession. When it comes to a choice between putting her name or her love affair with Troilus 'in jupartye', there is (as we shall see) no question in her mind about which to choose.

The supreme irony in the development of Criseyde's character is that in thus trying to preserve her 'name' she adopts the course of action that ultimately leads to her losing her 'name of trouthe in love for evermo' (V. 1055). That is how she puts it. But her disillusioned lover states the fact without any particularising adjunct:

> 'Who shal now trowe on any othes mo? ...
>   allas, youre name of trouthe
> Is now forlorn, and that is al my routhe.'
>   (V. 1681—87)

When rejecting Troilus's plan for elopement, she had declared:

> 'Ne though I lyvede *unto the worldes ende,*
> My *name* sholde I nevere ayeynward wynne;
> Thus were I lost, and that were routhe and synne.'
>   (IV. 1580—82)

In the speech in which she laments the loss of her 'name of trouthe in love', Chaucer introduces a verbal echo that underlines the irony of her behaviour:

> 'Allas, of me, *unto the worldes ende,*
> Shal neyther ben ywriten nor ysonge
> No good word; for thise bokes wol me shende.'
>   (V. 1058—60)

And so, unto Chaucer's day, 'Hire name, allas, is punysshed so wide' (V. 1085), being 'published' — to adopt the alternative reading found in some manuscripts — in the traditional Legend of Bad Women. Though Chaucer had no conceptual knowledge of Aristotle's principle of *peripeteia,* he has here created a telling instance of it.

The fact that Criseyde's punishment is exacted in the volatile House of Fame rather than the adamantine 'put of helle' allows the poet to offer some alleviation. In his earlier allegorical poem on Fame, Chaucer had shown how conscious he was of the poet's responsibility to the shades of the departed in the matter of preserving their true reputation or 'name' — particularly in preserving the reputation of famous and infamous lovers. The principal minstrels and 'gestiours' from the time of Orpheus onwards occupy niches on the exterior walls of Fame's castle; and on pillars within her hall stand the major 'auctoures' — the poets and chroniclers who have sustained the 'fame' of the heroes and heroines of former times. The fame of the Trojans is borne up, not only

by 'the gret Omer', but also by Chaucer's alleged ancient source for
Troilus and Criseyde, the mysterious Lollius, besides two of his actual,
indirect sources – the pseudo-Dares and the more recent 'Guydo ... de
Columpnis' (*HoF*, 1464–69). Chaucer goes on to tell how 'I gan ful wel
espie' a certain enmity between these 'authorities':

> Oon seyde that Omer made lyes,
> Feynynge in hys poetries,
> And was to Grekes favorable;
> Therfor held he hyt but fable.
> (1477–80)

If the testimony of reputable historical authorities can be so partial and
contentious, it is hardly surprising that Fame's distribution of good and
evil reputation to her various companies of clients should be as arbitrary
as the dealings of her sister, Fortune (cf. *HoF*, 1544–48).

In *The House of Fame* Chaucer does not go so far as to illustrate the
poet's power to affect the established reputation of a particular
individual, but he must have known one outstanding illustration of this
power in medieval literature. The principal figure in *Inferno* XIII is Piero
delle Vigne, Frederick II's chancellor, who, after serving his master
faithfully for twenty years, was accused of treason, blinded and
imprisoned where he is said to have dashed out his brains on the wall of
his cell. In his speech to Dante and Virgil he declares emphatically and
passionately that he was never traitor to his beloved lord; and he
requests them:

> 'E se di voi alcun nel mondo riede,
> conforti la memoria mia, che giace
> ancor del colpo che'nvidia le diede.'[4]

Piero had, in terms of *The House of Fame,* been included in the
second company of clients who throng the goddess's presence chamber:
those who deserved 'good fame', but were the victims of universal
slander. Dante uses his poetic authority to retrieve Piero's good name
from the damage done to it by Envy – though, with characteristic
irony, leaves him in Hell as a suicide.[5] 'Thise bokes', from which
Criseyde expects to receive no mercy, had placed her, in effect, among
the eighth company of clients: those who had 'ydoon the trayterye'
(*HoF*, 1812) and were rewarded with an infamous reputation – not
because Fame has any regard for justice, but simply because the
whimsical goddess was not disposed to grant their petition for a good
name. The goddess's notoriously arbitrary behaviour affords a sufficient
reason for the responsible and responsive poet to review Criseyde's
story. So Chaucer snatches the black, evil-smelling trumpet of
'Sklaundre' from the lips of Eolus; but there could be no question of his
substituting the golden clarion of 'Clere Laude'. In its different way,
Chaucer's treatment of Criseyde manifests a sympathy as unsentimental

as that to be seen in Dante's treatment of Piero. He performs the most charitable service to her memory of which the creative imagination is capable without distorting the received 'facts' of her history. This service consists of engaging all his poetic powers to demonstrate throughout the length of his poem how insubstantial is the surviving shadow compared with the human being who cast it.

Although the poet directs out sympathies primarily to the suffering and faithful hero, and although the narrative concludes with Troilus's solitary apotheosis, the story of Criseyde is hardly less affecting. In the following chapters I shall consider how the central interest of the poem lies in its exploration of the attempt by two human souls to establish the deepest and most searching of relationships. But the poet's representation of this relationship involves something more than a dialogue: the demands of love impose a rigorous dialectic that worries out the true nature of their personalities. Although their voices blend or complement each other antiphonally in the love-duet of Book III, they are heard in almost acrimonious debate in the concluding scene of Book IV. The contrast between these two scenes is itself part of a wider dialectic that induces a searching anatomy of love itself. The generalised notion of love is diffracted into a living spectrum of differing but merging attitudes embodied in the various *dramatis personae:* and the narrative of human intercourse is poised between a prologue that declares allegiance to the cult, over which Venus and her son preside, and an epilogue that affirms the only true source of love to be the religion of Christ and his mother.

Chapter Two
Epiphanies of the Beloved

It is not only the principal male characters within the narrative who cast Criseyde for the role of heroine in romances of their own devising; the poetry also encourages the reader himself to regard her in this way. Although Chaucer presents Criseyde, hardly less than Troilus, as a centre of consciousness (like a character in a modern novel) and causes her to contribute to a continually shifting dialectic (as in a drama), he pays sufficient deference to the conventions of romance to introduce her (no less than Emilye in *The Knight's Tale*) into the narrative proper as an apparently inaccessible object of surpassing beauty who inspires love at first sight. The literary vehicle that he employs for this purpose is the rhetorical *descriptio* beloved by the authors of the twelfth-century *Artes Poeticae* and by many an author of lyric and romance.[6] Whereas Emilye, who is generally content to allow others to arrange her life for her, remains almost identical with her introductory portrait (*CT.* I. 1035–55), Criseyde is not so easily epitomised. Indeed, her biographer is obliged to commission several portraits of her in order to keep pace with the developing action. Moreover, these portraits, upon close inspection, may appear to come from the hands of different artists.[7]

Troilus is granted his apotheosis, very properly, at the story's end and after the end of his life on earth, when he looked down from the Ogdoad, and, *ipso facto,* 'gan despise' the vanity of earthly life. But Criseyde, who never reaches the end of the story and disappears even before her death into the murky backward and abysm of infamy, is vouchsafed hers at I. 99–105 when she is likened to a 'hevenyssh perfit creature' sent down to earth 'in scornynge of nature'. The main difference is that, whereas the part of the hero that achieves apotheosis is his 'goost' (the aspect that a writer of a formal *descriptio* would discuss in the *notatio* or description of inner qualities of character), it is Criseyde's external beauty (the aspect of her that would have been included in an *effictio*) that is seen as supernatural in origin:

> Criseyde was this lady name al right;
> As to my doom, in al Troies cite
> Nas non so fair; for, passynge every wight,
> So angelik was hir natif beaute,
> That lik a thyng immortal semed she,
> As is an hevenyssh perfit creature,

That down were sent in scornynge of nature.

Hers is the kind of beauty that is apt to make 'Platonists' of men and to persuade them that it is a piece of perfection descended to earth and is capable of raising them to some transcendent region. An unspoken assumption of this 'sacramental' attitude is that her beauty must be the outward sign of an inward perfection of character. This attitude is common enough in European secular love-lyrics of the twelfth and thirteenth centuries; but in Chaucer's works it is unusual.[8]

The two concluding lines of the stanza, which particularly encourage us to take such a view of Criseyde, are Chaucer's addition to Boccaccio's statement that she was so fair, and so like an angel to look at, that she seemed not to be a mortal creature. Conventional medieval descriptions of paragons of female beauty often included a reference to the handiwork of Nature: Chaucer's usual practice is to declare that the subject of his *effictio* was that goddess's masterpiece. References to Nature may be seen, for example, in *The Book of the Duchess* (871–72), in *Anelida and Arcite* (78–80), and in *The Parlement of Foules* (372–78). The most extended example occurs in the portrait of Virginia, the fourteen-year-old heroine of *The Physician's Tale,* where a prosopopoeia – or speaking personification – of the goddess is introduced to add her own testimony to the narrator's assertion that

> Nature hath with sovereyn diligence
> Yformed hire in so greet excellence.
> *(CT.* VI. 9–10)

In her speech she asserts the superiority of her creative work to that of even the finest human artists:

> ...'Lo! I, Nature,
> Thus kan I forme and peynte a creature,
> Whan that me liste; who kan me countrefete?
> Pigmalion noght, though he may forge and bete,
> Or grave, or peynte; for I dar wel seyn,
> Apelles, Zanzis, sholde werche in veyn
> Outher to grave, or peynte, or forge, or bete,
> If they presumed me to countrefete.'
>
> (11–18)

But she acknowledges, nevertheless, that, as a creator, she is subordinate to God, the 'formere principal', for whom she acts (in accordance with a tradition that may be traced back through *The Parlement of Foules* and the *Roman de la Rose* to Alain of Lille and the School of Chartres) as 'vicaire general' in the matter of creating the physical part of man:

> 'For He that is the formere principal
> Hath maked me his vicaire general,
> To forme and peynten erthely creaturis

Right as me list, and ech thyng in my cure is
Under the moone, that may wane and waxe;
And for my werk right no thyng wol I axe;
My lord and I been ful of oon accord.
I made hire to the worshipe of my lord;
So do I alle myn othere creatures,
What colour that they han, or what figures.'
(19–29)

I have quoted this passage at length, and have referred to others, in
order to show how striking is the claim Chaucer makes for Criseyde's
beauty; it is as far above that of the finest creations of Nature as the
beauty of other secular heroines, themselves Nature's masterpieces, is
beyond the conception of the finest human artists. Such praise is the
proper prerogative only of spiritual beings or personfied qualities, such
as the Lady Reason in the *Roman de la Rose,* whose beauty is the
immediate creation of God without any delegation to Nature:

Hir goodly semblaunt, by devys,
I trowe were maad in paradys;
For Nature hadde nevere such a gras,
To forge a work of such compas.
For certeyn, but if the letter ly,
God hymself, that is so high,
Made hir after his ymage,
And yaff hir sith sich avauntage
That she hath myght and seignorie
To kepe men from all folye.
(*The Romaunt of the Rose,* 3205–14)

– which is hardly what Criseyde does.

In the same tradition are the lines in *Pearl* where the dreamer asks
the maiden – his own beloved daughter who is now a blessed spirit in
heaven:

'Quo formed þe þy fayre fygure?
Þat wroȝt þy wede, he watȝ ful wys.
Þy beaute com neuer of nature;
Pymalyon paynted neuer þy vys,
Ne Arystotel nawþer by hys lettrure
Of carped þe kynde þese properteȝ.
Þy colour passes þe flour-de-lys;
Þyn angel-hauyng so clene corteȝ ...'[9]

Curiously enough, these lines come nearer than any of the Chaucerian
passages to the description of Criseyde with her 'angelik' beauty that
made her seem like a 'thyng immortal' and a 'hevenyssh perfit creature'
sent down to earth 'in scornynge of nature'. The child in *Pearl*[10] is

regarded by the poet as an agent for his salvation. His deployment of
the image of the pearl seems to imply that she was sent down to earth
in order to attach his love so that, when God withdrew her to heaven,
his love would follow her thither to be transformed into a longing for
possession of the true pearl of great price: namely, what theologians call
the *summum bonum*. The function of the pearl-maiden in this poem is
in some ways analogous to that of Beatrice, whose beauty excited in
Dante a 'heavenly passion' which inspired him, after she had herself
become 'an hevenyssh perfit creature', to adopt her as his guide through
the celestial realm until she gives place — at two removes — to the figure
of the Virgin and he experiences the Beatific Vision. The 'yonge, fresshe
folkes' of Chaucer's audience could not forget for long that the Virgin,
who is invoked in the poem's final line, was the perfect exemplar of
feminine beauty and that the only lasting satisfaction of 'romantic'
longing was with Christ and his mother. The responsibilities of one
endowed with such a heavenly beauty as Criseyde's are great indeed.

If we look more closely at the language of this initial *effictio* of
Criseyde, we notice a certain tentativeness and evasiveness that subtly
undermine the idealising process. The statement that Criseyde's beauty
was 'so angelik' sounds confident enough, but the following line claims
no more than that '*lik* a thyng immortal *semed* she'. Moreover, the word
lik here acts retrospectively upon the *angelik* of the previous line. This
word is properly derived from a Latin *angelicus* and so its lexical
meaning is 'possessing the qualities of an angel'. This also appears to be
its contextual meaning until we reach the 'lik' of the next line, which
insinuates into our minds the suggestion that the derivation may be
'angel-like'. So the power of the confident assertion is diminished and
the work of reduction begun by *lik* in line 103 is continued by the
tentative *As* of line 104, which introduces the stanza's concluding
statement. Similarly, by the time we reach the final line the confident
was of line 102 has given place to the subjunctive *were* (though some
manuscripts read *was*). Moreover, the strict semasiologist in us may be
disconcerted by a 'natif beaute' that is said to be superior to 'nature'.
And we have yet to consider the full implications of 'scornynge'.

As soon as we set the description in its narrative context, we find
that the angel's wings have been shorn off: the one by Heredity, the
other by Environment. Her father has proved to be a turncoat who, in
order to save his skin, is even prepared to leave his own flesh and blood
behind him in a city that he knows to be doomed. A far less strenuous
exercise in the art of 'calkulynge' than that which enabled Calkas to
foresee that 'Troye sholde / Destroyed ben' would have sufficed for him
to realise that, after his departure, the Trojans would declare that

> ... he and al his kyn at ones
> Ben worthi for to brennen, fel and bones.

(I. 90—91)

22

Criseyde is made to seem even more vulnerable, in the hostile environment to which she has been abandoned, from the fact that

> ... bothe a widewe was she and allone
> Of any frend to whom she dorste hir mone.
>
> (I. 97–98)

In spite of being almost overcome by 'sorwe and fere', she shows some initiative and courage in going straight to Hector to ask for protection. Yet, even after this has been granted, her position in the city remains a delicate one, as may be seen from the ease with which Pandarus later gains credibility for his fabrication about Polyphete's supposed lawsuit against her. Indeed, at the critical moment, even Hector's championing of her cannot prevent the 'parlement' from trading her (as a make-weight to King Thoas) for Antenor.

Such is her situation when her second epiphany is vouchsafed to us — or, rather, to Troilus. For, whereas, in the earlier description of her, the reader is made to experience something of her seemingly supernatural aura, while at the same time being made aware of her human limitations, at her second manifestation there is irony in that her supernatural aspects perform their magical offices upon Troilus, while the privileged reader is helped to analyse her 'epiphany' in psychological and circumstantial terms.

When Criseyde is first seen at the Feast of Palladion emphasis is placed upon the social context. We are not surprised to be told concerning the angelic paragon of the earlier description that 'Hire goodly lokyng gladede al the prees' (I. 173). But her beauty is no longer seen as being different in kind from that of other women. The simile that Chaucer now applies to it concedes priority to her while placing her in a mortal series:

> Right as oure firste lettre is now an A,
> In beaute first so stood she makeles.
>
> (I. 171–72)

But if — as seems likely — a passing compliment to Queen Anne is implied in this alphabetical simile, then Criseyde is still being set somewhat apart from the others; her superiority is not merely that of the first lady of the land. The comparative dowdiness of the other ladies of the congregation shares with her black widow's habit the function of acting as a foil to set off her matchless beauty:

> Nas nevere yit seyn thyng to ben preysed derre,
> Nor under cloude blak so bright a sterre.
>
> (I. 174–75)

Nor is this the only suggestion in the stanza that her widowhood, which previously made her a helpless and pathetic object, is a potential source of strength. The other is in line 172, where the epithet 'makeles', by virtue of a piece of word-play found elsewhere in Middle English poetry, may not only indicate that her beauty was peerless, but may also allude to the fact that she happens not to be tied to any 'make' and may therefore be available for love.[11]

This stanza, which presents such an idealised and romantic view of the lady, is followed by — and syntactically linked to — one that presents her in naturalistic terms. She may, in the scale of aesthetic values, have stood out in front of other women; but, as a matter of narrative fact, her physical location in the temple was just the opposite:

> And yit she stood ful lowe and stille allone,
> Byhynden other folk in litel brede,
> And neigh the dore, ay under shames drede ...
>
> (I. 178–80)

The difference in attitude of the two stanzas is epitomised in the contrast between the exalted 'makeles' of line 172, with its suggestive, secondary connotation in train, and the corresponding 'allone' of line 178, which is flat, unhopeful, and pinned into position by its phonic association with 'lowe'. In the stanza's penultimate line the description changes direction yet again. Though 'simple of atire' refers properly to the decent habiliments of widowhood, it may also suggest the eulogy of Horace's 'simplex munditiis' (*Odes* I, v. 5). In the second half of the line Criseyde is described as 'debonaire of chere' and in the final line she stands 'with ful assured lokyng and manere'.

This peculiar 'lokyng' of Criseyde will constitute the metaphorical arrow with which Cupid brings about the subjugation of 'This Troilus' — who makes his first entrance into the narrative proper at the beginning of the very next line (I. 183). In case we should disregard the importance of this look, Chaucer underlines it for us throughout the remainder of the temple scene (cf. I. 229–31; 295–96; 306–7), as Troilus returns home (I. 325), and as he sits day-dreaming on his bed (I. 363–64). The lover still recalls it in Book III, when Criseyde lies naked in his arms and he kisses the eyes from which the glance issued (1338 [1352] – 1344 [1359]). Moreover, the look is carefully analysed when the second description of Criseyde is resumed at I. 281–94 after the narration of Cupid's revenge upon Troilus.

The first stanza of the resumed description looks superficially like a straightforward, itemised *effictio*. But its expression is curiously negative. Instead of declaring, as he later does (V. 806), that 'Criseyde mene was of hire stature' (i.e. 'of medium height'), he states that 'She nas nat with the leste of hire stature'. Similarly, instead of saying that she was 'very feminine', he declares:

> But alle hire lymes so wel answerynge
> Weren to wommanhode, that creature

Nas nevere lasse mannyssh in semynge.
(I. 282–84)

What is meant by 'wommanhode' is defined more positively in the stanza's final line as: 'Honour, estat, and wommanly noblesse'. In spite of the facts alleged in the earlier part of the stanza, the general impression it gives is of a Junoesque presence and nobility as much as of Venereal seductiveness and femininity.

It is the Junoesque quality that particularly attracts Troilus; as the second stanza of the description indicates:

> To Troilus right wonder wel with alle
> Gan for to like hire mevynge and hire chere,
> Which somdel deignous was; for she let falle
> Hire look a lite aside, in swich manere
> Ascaunces, 'what? may I nat stonden here?'
> And after that hir lokynge gan she lighte,
> That nevere thoughte hym seen so good a syghte.
> (I. 288–94)

The disdainful expression certainly befits a goddess; but what so affects Troilus is the transition of this 'chere' into a lighter glance. Troilus experiences the thrill of seeing the clouds pass from the brow of a proud and inaccessible goddess to reveal a tender woman. This is characteristic of the impression of her that is mirrored in his mind throughout the poem. It is stated most explicitly at I. 425–26 when, in an apostrophe to Cupid, he asks:

> 'But wheither goddesse or womman, iwis,
> She be, I not, which that ye do me serve.'

But the reader already knows enough about her to guess that the reason for her defiant expression is defensive. It is her reaction to what she imagines many Trojans are thinking about the presence of a traitor's daughter in their midst, just as, in *The Reeve's Tale,* the wife of 'deynous Symkyn' is as *'digne* as water in a dich' because of her awareness of being 'somdel smoterliche' on account of her parentage (*CT.* I. 3963 ff).[12]

In spite of this psychological explanation, the 'deignous' glance also appears to be germane to her peculiar beauty. It looks back, through the 'ful assured lokyng and manere' of I. 182, to the 'natif beaute ... *scornynge* of nature' described when she is first introduced. This element of aristocratic disdain in her beauty makes her, in one respect, a suitable match for Troilus, who is introduced as a 'fierse and proude knyght' who scorns love (I. 232–34) and 'scorned hem that loves peynes dryen' (I. 303). Indeed, when the narrator first refers to his presumptuous scorning of love, it is seen as almost equivalent to scorning 'kynde' or nature (I. 232–38). There is an obvious parallel between Criseyde's 'deignous' expression that caused her to let fall

> Hire look a lite aside, in swich manere
> *Ascaunces,* 'what? may I nat stonden here?'
> (I. 291–92)

and the account of Troilus's supercilious gesture when he congratulates himself on his scornful address to his love-lorn companions:

> And with that word he gan caste up the browe,
> *Ascaunces,* 'loo! is this nat wisely spoken?'
> (I. 204–05)

A less obvious way in which the natural compatibility of hero and heroine is suggested is in the depth of penetration of their 'lokynge'. Troilus's gaze passes unaffected across the countenances of the ladies who enthrall the hearts of his companions and pierces through the ranks of worshippers until it meets the beauty and the carefully described 'lokyng' of Criseyde, which (all unconsciously) lies in wait for it:

> Withinne the temple he wente hym forth pleyinge,
> This Troilus, of every wight aboute,
> On this lady, and now on that, lokynge,
> Where so she were of towne or of withoute,
> And upon cas bifel that thorugh a route
> His eye percede, and so depe it wente,
> Til on Criseyde it smot, and ther it stente.
> (I. 267–73)

But the depths through which Criseyde's look (unconsciously) penetrates are within Troilus himself:

> And of hire look in him ther gan to quyken
> So gret desir, and swiche affeccioun,
> That in his hertes botme gan to stiken
> Of hir his fixe and depe impressioun.
> (I. 295–98)

In this second description of Criseyde, then, the most striking visual feature is the way in which the poet, with the art of a subtle portrait-painter, captures a fleeting, but characteristic expression of his subject by depicting her countenance as the 'deignous' look melts into a lighter glance. The goddess-like epiphany is offset and framed by her widow's attire ('Nor under cloude blak so brighte a sterre'), with its delimiting and humanising implications, and her sideways glance is further framed by the 'route', which lends it perspective depth as it is projected towards Troilus's innermost heart. The reader is told just enough about the heroine's true plight to enable him to appreciate something of the irony of the developing situation. But for a full appreciation of this irony we have to wait until Book II, where the character of the girl who has been presented as a paradigm of supernatural beauty is gradually unfolded in an action whose mimetic milieu is that of domestic comedy.

On the third occasion when Chaucer ventures to describe his heroine she is portrayed as a nude:

> Hire armes smale, hire streyghte bak and softe,
> Hire sydes longe, flesshly, smothe, and whit
> He gan to stroke, and good thrift bad ful ofte
> Hire snowissh throte, hire brestes rounde and lite:
> Thus in this hevene he gan him to delite ...
>
> (III. 1247–51)

Despite the frankness of the description, there is no hint of prurience in these lines — which is more than can be said of the corresponding moment in Canto III of *Il Filostrato* where Criseida, having stripped herself to her last garment, pauses to utter a speech of coy, reluctant, amorous delay. Again, the innocent nakedness of Chaucer's Criseyde is far removed from the posture of the degraded Venus in the sultry and sinister temple of brass in *The Parlement of Foules*, who is discovered in the half-light half-naked:

> ... and, sothly for to say,
> The remnaunt was wel kevered to my pay,
> Ryght with a subtyl coverchef of Valence —
> Ther nas no thikkere cloth of no defense.
>
> (270–73)

The innocence of Criseyde's nakedness is further emphasised by the fact that, from the beginning of the scene, she has been asleep in her naked bed, as was customary in Chaucer's day. Nor is Troilus allowed to throw off his clothes in an ecstasy of expected pleasure, but has to suffer the comic indignity of being stripped, while unconscious, by Pandarus, for medical reasons.

The description of the naked Criseyde in these lines is certainly stylised: the reference to the lady's smooth sides, for example, was so common a feature of medieval *effictiones* that in the opening stanza of *Pearl,* when the author wishes to conform the likeness of a baby girl to that of a pearl, he says, 'So smale, so smoþe hyr sydeȝ were'. So it might be assumed that the final line of the passage just quoted ('Thus in this hevene he gan him to delite') is likewise no more than a piece of conventional amatory hyperbole, were it not that religious metaphors are used consistently and pointedly throughout the whole of this episode. In the opening line of the very next stanza occurs one of the boldest of these adaptations of the language of Christianity to the ecstasies of Erotic love, when Troilus addresses Cupid as ' "O Love, O Charite ..." ' (III. 1254). The word 'hevene' also refers us back to Criseyde's first epiphany, for the 'hevenyssh, perfit creature' who was

sent down to earth 'in scornynge of nature' now lies enclosed in
Troilus's caressing arms; the eyes from which proceeded the glance that
penetrated his heart are now *'humble* nettes' subject to his kisses (III.
1339–41 [1353–55]). Criseyde has come down to Earth in order that
Troilus might be raised up to Heaven: indeed, he now believes that he is
joined to her by the love that binds in harmony the whole of creation
(III. 1261 – an idea that is expanded in III. 1744–71). The formerly
remote goddess, who first manifested herself to him in the temple,
where she was shrouded in inaccessibility, now reveals all the mystery of
her beauty to him, palpably and tangibly.

In spite of the assertive, religious language, the tone of the
description and of much of its context forbids us to indulge in
unrestrained flights of Platonic ecstasy as we contemplate this particular
incarnation of Beauty. There is no question of Chaucer's here
anticipating the Renaissance convention that Venus, when painted nude,
represents Celestial rather than natural love. Indeed, the conventions of
the medieval *effictio* hardly endow Criseyde with the classical
proportions of a Renaissance Venus, but rather the elongated figure of a
Gothic depiction of Eve, who represents female humanity, not idealised
femininity; the 'fresshe, womanliche wif' of III. 1296, in fact.

The lines that describe the naked Criseyde, then, blend the idea of
the incarnate goddess with that of the vulnerable daughter of Eve. A
similar blend of superiority and vulnerability is also evident in the
account of her behaviour in the immediate context of the description –
a perpetuation of the ambivalent attitude that characterised the portraits
of Criseyde in Book I. When Troilus embraces her, 'Right as an aspes
leef she gan to quake' (III 1200). Yet, when he tells her that she is
caught and demands her surrender, her reply,[13] though tender and
compliant, asserts her sovereignty and makes it clear that she regards
herself as ultimately in control. Even when the 'humble nettes' of her
eyes are subject to his kisses, her expression retains something of that
'deignous' power which enthralled him in the temple scene and which
continues to baffle him now:

> 'Ye humble nettes of my lady deere.
> Though ther be mercy writen in youre cheere,
> God woot the text ful hard is, soth, to fynde:
> How coude ye withouten bond me bynde?'
>   (III. 1341–44 [1355–58])

Earlier in the Book it is stated that Troilus became for her a 'wal / Of
steel' (III. 479–80) on account of his model discretion. Yet, when
Criseyde admonishes him for his supposed jealousy, she sounds almost
maternal:

> 'Wol ye the childissh jalous contrefete?

28

Now were it worthi that ye were ybete.'
(III. 1168—69)

However, Troilus does not regard her so much as a 'mother-surrogate'[14]
as an embodiment of the Eternal Feminine that draws us above. He
believes that she has been ordained by God to guide him in the paths of
virtue:

'And, for the love of god, my lady deere,
Syn god hath wrought me for I shal yow serve, —
As thus I mene, he wol ye be my steere,
To do my lyve, if that yow list, or sterve, —
So techeth me how that I may deserve
Youre thonk, so that I, thorugh myn ignoraunce,
Ne do no thyng that do yow displesaunce.'
(III. 1289—95)

In these lines she becomes almost a pagan counterpart of Beatrice. Later
we are told that Troilus's love causes him to feel in his life 'a newe
qualitee' (III. 1654), as if Criseyde had inaugurated for him a veritable
Vita Nuova.

The supernatural-seeming beauty that emanates from her eyes is still
remembered in the fourth and final description of Criseyde
(V. 806—26):

Lo, trewely, they writen that hire syen,
That paradis stood formed in hire eyen.
(V. 816—17)

Moreover, editors have observyd that V. 817 is reminiscent of *Paradiso,*
xviii, 21, where Beatrice makes a similar statement about her own eyes.
But in the present context the allusion to paradise is sadly ironical. For
the portrait occurs at the point where Criseyde is about to yield to one
who has no interest in the transcendental possibilities of love — it is
appropriately placed between formal portraits of this new lover and the
old one. Formally this description of Criseyde differs from those in the
earlier books in that, after two stanzas of *effictio,* it adds a third
devoted to *notatio.* Into this final stanza the poet inserts the celebrated
criticism of Criseyde as 'slydynge of corage' (V. 825). This is not the
only feature of this final portrait that may incline us to believe that
here at last subjective 'epiphanies' have yielded to objective revelation.

The statement that she was 'slydynge of corage' is smuggled into the
notatio in much the same way as discreditable facts about the
Canterbury pilgrims are often introduced into portraits in the *General
Prologue.* It follows close upon the heels of a five-and-a-half-line
procession of eulogistic epithets and panegyrical phrases; and the
consequent 'indiscretion' is hastily covered up by the chiming intrusion
of the inconsequential final line: 'But, trewely, I kan nat telle hire age'.

But an even more disturbing instance of the poet's smuggling in of an unflattering detail has already occurred in the *effictio* itself. The first stanza begins by repeating information about Criseyde's physical stature that was vouchsafed to us in Book I, continues with some generalised praise of her beauty, and concludes with an account of her favourite coiffure — a trivial detail not previously mentioned. Not so trivial is another new detail that is introduced in a deceptively complacent manner at the beginning of the next stanza:

> And save hire browes joyneden yfere,
> Ther nas no lakke, in aught I kan espien.
>
> (V. 813–14)

The degree of this blemish should not be exaggerated; Chaucer is not suggesting that, after all, she was *une jolie laide*. Nevertheless, the revelation so late in the narrative that the 'hevenyssh, perfit creature' has any physical blemish at all administers an even greater shock than the statement in the following stanza about her being 'slydynge of corage' — for we have been told about her treachery from the beginning of the poem.[15] It is all the more surprising that nothing has been said previously about this feature when we recall how carefully Criseyde's appearance has been analysed — at a distance and in close-up, in outline and in particulars, clothed and naked — and especially when we remember the repeated attention paid to her eyes that are so unaesthetically linked by the offending brows. Indeed, immediately after mentioning the blemish, the poet (as we have seen) almost succeeds in casting the old spell once more by evoking the image of paradise that 'stood formed in hire eyen'. But the damage has been done: the fact that this angelic beauty has a 'lakke' cannot now be forgotten. And when this very word occurs again during the *notatio* — even though it is as another part of speech and negatived — the reader's suspicions are alerted. Instead of stating that she was full of pity, Chaucer writes: 'Ne nevere mo ne lakked hire pite' (V. 825). We are impelled to wonder, half unconsciously: what, then, was lacking in her character? And we receive an answer as the reference to 'pite' slides into the next line where the approving epithet 'tendre-herted' is converted with such disconcerting facility into the deprecating phrase 'slydynge of corage'.

We should pause, however, before accepting this portrait as the heroine's authentic likeness and before relegating the other pictures to the attic as romantic falsifications. It is well known that this portrait (like those of Diomede and Troilus by which it is flanked) is based upon formal descriptions from sources older than *Il Filostrato* — Boccaccio at the more or less corresponding point offers a brief description of Diomede only. These descriptions are inserted into the narrative as if they were documents that Chaucer has just discovered in his archive and which he now offers for the reader's inspection. When a twentieth-century reader first encounters them, his experience may remind him of coming across, at page 534 of a biography of an eminent Victorian, a set of primitive photographs that give only a hint of the personality which the biographer has brought to life with subtlety and insight, and the position of which seems to have been determined by the binder rather than the author.

But the positioning of these portraits is part of the poem's strategy: this description of Criseyde occurs, in one sense, too late and, in another, too soon. A further comparison with the *General Prologue* will make this clear. Whereas the portraits of the Canterbury pilgrims are introductory (their characters often being developed later in the work), this one of Criseyde is reductionist: all the living complexity and variety of behaviour and personality that has flowered throughout three-and-a-half books is now simplified to what can be accommodated within three stanzas. Again, whereas the vignettes of the pilgrims have something of the relaxed air of a gossip column, the judicial and summary manner of this account of Criseyde gives it the ominous character of an obituary notice published prematurely. The description is, in fact, urging us away from the woman, whom Chaucer's imagination has re-created, towards the shadow that survived in the House of Fame. It is therefore essential that we keep all four of her portraits on view in our mental gallery. As we look upon this picture and on this, we may find ourselves repeating a couplet from Pope's essay on the Characters of Women:

How many pictures of one nymph we view,
And how unlike each other, all how true!
(*Moral Essays,* II. 5–6)

Chapter Three
The Operators

Insofar as Criseyde is represented in this externalised way, she will appear, within the elementary syntax of love's conventional grammar, as the object, the mere sight of whom excites what Theseus, in *The Knight's Tale,* calls 'al this hoote fare' (*CT.* I. 1809). Troilus is the subject of whom the action purports to be predicated: 'The double sorwe of Troilus to tellen ...'. But he is a subject more passive than active: he is pursued more than he pursues — his pursuer being (as already observed) the vindictive god of love bent upon revenge for the prince's taunting of him and his votaries. Yet it is a compliment to Troilus's noble and refined nature that Cupid thinks him worth his most subtle and prolonged attentions: Diomede, though he has the god much in his mouth, falls quite beneath his notice.

The Verbal function is performed by the 'operators', Pandarus and Diomede: the role of the one being to convert idealised potentiality into physical act by bringing the lovers together; that of the other to subvert idealism by wrenching them finally apart. It is true that Diomede desires the girl for himself; but we hear little of him after he has won Criseyde. His main function in the plot is to act as a very efficient machine for unpicking Troy and Troilus from her mind so that they 'shal knotteles throughout hire herte slide' (V. 769).

Although this predatory youth does not appear until Book V, it will be convenient to consider him first, as he is the least complicated of all the principal *dramatis personae.* On the two occasions (V. 92–105; 771–98) when we are permitted to enter into his secret thoughts it is merely to hear him formulate a resolve which he promptly proceeds to execute; no shadow of frustration falls between his desires and their fulfilment. But, although we see only a very small part of the action through his eyes, his very presence in the poem represents an attitude towards the whole narrative of love which, however unwelcome, cannot be ignored. His presence encourages us to look at the action of what purports to be a romance of *fine amour* from the irreverent point of view of a market analyst, rather than from the sympathetic point of view of a psycho-analyst.

The report of such an economist will bluntly state that, whereas Troilus, even with the very considerable assistance of a cunning go-between, takes three long books to win the girl, Diomede is represented as winning her unaided in the course of only a few stanzas.

In terms of a 'cost-benefit' analysis or a 'time and emotion' study, Diomede certainly appears to secure the greater return for effort expended. These brutal statistics imply a criticism of Troilus: the obverse of that criticism of Diomede that sees him as a degraded replica of the courtly hero.[16]

Devotees of romance will object that Diomede does not play the game according to the rules. Such readers will not need the authority of Andreas Capellanus to point out to them that a man who makes advances to a lady, when he knows her heart to be plighted elsewhere, is no true servant of Love;[17] for in the demesne of *fine amour* where, as often as not, relationships lack the legal sanction of marriage, the understanding that governs all such contracts is: 'our word is our bond' — for ever. Bur Diomede knows from Calchas's 'calkulynge' that Troy is doomed; and, so, any lover Criseyde may have in that 'prisoun' is virtually dead already. This, indeed, is an argument that he employs when trying to eradicate the memory of Troilus from her heart (V. 876–924); according to his point of view, he is merely being 'realistic'. But he is also being dishonest with himself as well as with Criseyde: Chaucer tells us elsewhere (V. 792–94) that what particularly made him determined to win her was the thought of conquering a rival. Moreover, the metaphors that Chaucer applies to him reveal his true attitude:

> This Diomede, of whom yow telle I gan,
> Goth now withinne hym self ay arguynge
> How he may best, with shortest taryinge,
> Unto his net Criseydes herte brynge.
> To this entente he koude nevere fyne;
> To fisshen hire, he leyde out hook and lyne.
>
> (V. 771–77)

Counsel for Diomede, learned in the statute lore of 'courtly love', might remind us that, according to Andreas Capellanus himself, *amor* is derived from [h]*amus,* 'a hook'.[18] The Prosecution will, however, call in evidence not only the true principles of etymology, but the other metaphors of fishing in the poem. Those at II. 328 and III. 1161–62 imply a certain shiftiness on the part of the person to whom they are applied. But the most interesting occurs in a couplet from the narrator's hymn to Venus that begins Book III. Venus alone understands the mystery of why

> She loveth hym, or whi he loveth here, —
> As whi this fissh, and naught that, cometh to were.
>
> (III. 34–35)

The accidents of falling in love are, however, no sacred mystery to Diomede: with his 'hook and lyne' he pulls out the most succulent fish for himself.

Although Diomede does not play the game according to the rules, he gives a superficial impression of doing so. But his use of love's rhetoric slides too glibly off his 'tonge large':

'For though ye Troians with us Grekes wrothe
Han many a day ben, alwey yit, parde,
O god of love in soth we serven bothe.
And, for the love of god, my lady fre,
Whom so ye hate, as beth nat wroth with me.
For trewely, ther kan no wight yow serve,
That half so loth youre wrathe wolde deserve.'

(V. 141–47)

The simple chiasmus, 'love of god ... god of love', is the kind of smart figure — medieval rhetoricians called it *commutatio* — that such a gallant might well have used 'in real life' when 'chatting up' a prospective 'date'. But the poet heightens the impression of the speaker's practised smoothness by his patterning of sound: the argument circles round from the plural *wrothe* of 141 to the singular *wroth* of 145 and on to the substantival *wrathe* of 147 by way of the assonant *soth* and *bothe* (143) and *loth* (147); the development from 'we serven' (143) to 'yow serve' (146) reveals the same practised neatness of expression.

Similarly, the counterfeit character of Diomede's performance as a lover is exposed by means of Chaucer's exploitation of syntactical and metrical effects. The poet had described Troilus's declaration of love as follows:

In chaunged vois, right for his verray drede,
Which vois ek quook, and therto his manere
Goodly abaist, and now his hewes rede,
Now pale, unto Criseyde, his lady dere,
With look down cast, and humble iyolden chere,
Lo, thalderfirste word that hym asterte
Was, twyes: 'mercy, mercy, swete herte!'

And stynte a while and when he myghte out brynge,
The nexte word was ...

(III. 92–100)

All this hesitant 'chere' is entirely spontaneous (as the context also shows). But no doubt every expression and every gesture could have been studied from a treatise on *pronunciatio;* and, when Diomede uses them, they obviously have been. The impression of their having been picked out of a catalogue is conveyed by the poet's most elementary use of parataxis and the crudest possible deployment of anaphora: in short, every line begins with 'And':

And with that word he gan to waxen red,
And in his speche a litel wight he quook,

And caste asyde a litel wight his hed,
And stynte a while; and afterward he wook,
And sobreliche on hire he threw his look,
And seyde ...

(V. 925–30)

– And what he says, to clinch the stanza, consists of a boast about his lineage, as against Troilus's 'mercy, mercy, swete herte'.[19]

The artificiality of the performance is further betrayed by the repetition in consecutive lines of the phrase 'a litel wight' – which suggests the action of an automaton. The whole process is, in any case, too rapid. When Troilus's emotion forces him to pause, a new stanza is required to indicate the break; but Diomede merely pauses across the caesura at the very centre of the stanza before we are told: 'and afterward he wook' – where 'wook' is too strong a word to be taken seriously.

The discrepancy between rather too smooth courtly speech and grosser intentions, evident in the conduct of 'this sodeyn Diomede' (V. 1024), may be seen, taken to its final *reductio ad absurdum,* in the contrast between the 'courtly' speeches and the accompanying actions of 'hende Nicholas' in *The Miller's Tale.* Indeed, these two gallants might easily exchange titles: 'hende Diomede', in view of his smooth speeches and manners, and 'sodeyn Nicholas', in view of the manner of his first approach to his landlord's young wife (*CT.* I. 3276–78). It has been pointed out[20] that in this tale other senses of 'hende' are also operative; namely that of 'handy' – 'on the spot' and also 'too free with his hands'. The word is no less applicable to Diomede in these secondary senses. As an aristocrat, he cannot be permitted to express himself with the blatant crudity of the bourgeois clerk. But it is significant that the first favour he receives from Criseyde is not granted: it is snatched as a prize; he 'took her glove' (V. 1013) as nonchalantly as, two lines later, he 'took his leve'.

Even the concessions that Criseyde makes to him voluntarily read like a series of commercial gains. Chaucer compiles an inventory of these items, in apparently ascending order of value and conveniently compacted into two consecutive stanzas (V. 1037–50). The first stanza specifies two items that were formerly the property of Troilus: the bay steed and the brooch. It also mentions a third that had not, indeed, belonged to her discarded lover; but she more than gives it to Diomede: 'She *made hym were* a pencel of hire sleve'.

The second stanza is devoted entirely to describing how the ultimate favour was added to the list of spoils. Ironically it is when he is wounded by Troilus that this prince, who was so powerfully motivated by the desire of conquering a rival lover, finally triumphs:

... tho wepte she many a tere,
Whan that she saugh his wyde woundes blede;

And that she took to kepen hym good hede,
And for to hele hym of his sorwes smerte
Men seyn, I not, that she yaf hym hire herte.

(V. 1047—50)

Although Chaucer cannot bring himself to declare unequivocally that Criseyde ever had her heart in the transaction, he makes it clear that Diomede obtained exactly what he desired. Yet, at best, all that Diomede could hope to experience with Criseyde was what Troilo enjoyed with Criseida, once she had cast aside her last remaining garment:

D'amor sentiron l'ultimo valore'
[They experienced the ultimate gratification of love]

They could not hope to experience what Chaucer — perhaps through an inspired misunderstanding of Boccaccio — tells us that Troilus enjoyed with Criseyde:

... bitwixen drede and sikernesse,
They felte in love the grete worthynesse.

(III. 1315—16)

The presence of Diomede insinuates into the poem the cynical moral that the man who is most likely to win a lady's 'herte' for himself will be one who has no genuine feelings of *fine amour* or romantic love. A similar discrepancy between the act of loving and the art of winning a lady's love is implied, though in a more delicate and oblique way, in the behaviour of Pandarus. As a 'romantic' lover, he is unable to advance his own suit; but, as a proxy wooer, he is able to manipulate his niece into the role of Troilus's mistress. His avowed doctrine of love is the very opposite of Diomede's; indeed, it appears to place him even nearer than Troilus to the idealising end of love's spectrum. If Troilus appears to exemplify the ideals so eloquently expressed by the royal tercelet eagle in *The Parlement of Foules* (414—441), his friend abides by a code of conduct similar to that approved by the female turtle dove (582—588). We are told that for some time he has continued to 'serve' faithfully a lady, in spite of her having always remained 'straunge' towards him.

It is true that this affair is kept so far in the background that the lady never appears in person on this side of the poem's horizon. The fact that she is not one of the *dramatis personae* may tend to make us somewhat incredulous of this relationship; but we should observe that Troilus takes it very seriously (cf. I. 621—23 and IV. 484—90). Pandarus's devotion to this lady, who remains unkind to him and anonymous to us, must be seen as the principal part of the tribute he pays to Cupid in order to propitiate that masterful and vengeful deity. Unlike the immature Troilus, who scorned lovers and their 'lewed observaunces', he recognises the power of love and so has escaped the terrible nemesis visited upon his friend. We may perhaps be forgiven for suspecting that it is almost part of his strategy to fall in love with a lady who is 'out of his star'. Being aware, like the poem's narrator, of his 'unlikelynesse' as a performer in the dance of love, in which he will 'hoppe alwey byhynde' (II. 107), he settles for an object of admiration who is unlikely to return his passion. On to her he can project all his romantic fantasies and will think particularly of her on such days as the Third of May (II. 50—63), when the 'dismal' causes love melancholy to possess his soul; or as on the occasion when he beseeches Troilus (who has at last been admitted to his lady's grace):

> 'And bid for me, sith thow art now in blysse,
> That god me sende deth or soone lisse.'
> (III. 342—43)

But — again like the narrator — he finds an outlet for his frustrated erotic energy by acting as the servant of Love's servants in helping to bring about the consummation of the loves of a hero and heroine who are so well endowed with those very gifts of Nature that will make them 'likely' candidates for the direct service of Cupid. Through his indirect service, Pandarus makes up the full complement of the tribute demanded by the god.

This enforced celibacy seems to fit him for the metaphorical role of priest of Cupid and Venus. His sacerdotal function has often been noted, but it has implications that deserve further exploration. As soon as he learns that his formerly sceptical friend has been converted to his religion, he assumes the role of confessor (I. 932—45) and enthusiastically predicts that Troilus will become a pillar of Love's church: 'the beste post, I leve, / Of al his lay'.[21] He delightedly takes a whole stanza to make the point that the greatest heretics often prove to be the most zealous converts (I. 1002—08). When Criseyde eventually receives Troilus into her 'service', Pandarus falls on his knees in a prayer to Venus and Cupid (III. 183—89) which anticipates the devout language of Troilus's hymns later in Book III. His hovering officiousness on the lovers' behalf right up to the threshold of consummation may be interpreted as his ritual ministrations at the altar of Cupid. For his lingering presence in the bedroom cannot be accounted for in terms of either 'naturalistic' probability or literary precedent. Pandaro is entirely absent from the corresponding scene in Canto III of *Il Filostrato* and, as Professor Muscatine remarks: 'This is the first time in medieval literature that a go-between must go so far as actually to pick up the hero and throw him into the lady's bed'.[22] Nor can his role be completely accounted for in terms of the watchman traditionally associated with the singing of the *alba* or *tagelied*. Just as he remains too long for a go-between, so he performs 'too shortly [hys] offys' as watchman. Long before the lovers join in the singing of the antiphonal *aubade* he retires to sleep and does not re-appear until after Troilus's departure.

At times his office seems to invest him with almost daemonic energy, as if he were the embodiment of some kind of 'Life Force', like the personification Genius in the *Roman de la Rose*,[23] whose sole concern is to precipitate couples towards sexual union without any regard to the possibilities of spiritual, moral, or psychological communion. But, if he does represent any such force, then it is a sterilised 'life force' that he signifies. In the *Roman de la Rose* Genius is presented as the priest and confessor of Nature, who is herself the Creator's vicar in the physical realm; and so he regards *engendrure* as the sole justification for sexual relations. Pandarus serves at the altar of Cupid and Venus – not at Nature's forge. Like that other comic 'servant' of Venus, Chauntecleer – who performed his service 'more for delit than world to multiplye' (*CT.* VII. 3345) – he regards love as an end in itself.[24]

Few readers are likely to go so far as D. W. Robertson who, looking down from austere patristic heights upon this superficially 'attractive little man', sees him as nothing less than a 'priest of Satan'.[25] On the other hand, no one can regard his conduct – and especially his treatment of his niece – as wholly admirable. There is an element of casuistry in this self-ordained cleric. Seizing upon the commonplace that all men must suffer 'loves hete, / Celestial, or elles love of kynde' (I. 978–79), and having decided that Criseyde is not yet ready for celestial love, he convinces himself that:

> ... it sate hire wel right nowthe
> A worthi knyght to loven and cherice,
> And but she do, I holde it for a vice.'
> (I. 985–87)

But the priest's idealistic intentions for the lovers are inevitably contaminated by the nature of his office as go-between – about which he has scruples at certain moments (cf. II. 353; and his exchange with Troilus, III. 239–40). The process of contamination is revealed through the imagery in which his actions are depicted. When he undertakes to woo his niece on behalf of 'His fulle frende' he recognises that he is engaged upon an enterprise of some delicacy that will require much preparatory thought. In commending his circumspection the author introduces an architectural comparison:

> For everi wight that hath an hous to founde
> Ne renneth naught the werk for to bygynne
> With rakel hond; but he wol bide a stounde,
> And sende his hertes line out fro withinne
> Aldirfirst his purpos for to wynne.
> Al this Pandare in his herte thoughte,
> And caste his werk ful wisly or he wroughte.
> (I. 1065–71)

The comparison of him to the designer who eschews the stretching forth of 'rakel hond' to begin an enterprise certainly distinguishes him, for the moment, from 'this sodeyne Diomede'. Similarly, whereas the extrovert Greek sets out 'hook and line' to catch Criseyde, her uncle, at this point in the narrative, imitates the artist who pauses to 'sende his hertes line out fro withinne'. An even more important implication of the simile is that this pragmatist is also an idealist who takes a constructive view of the enterprise to which he has committed himself: the love relationship which he fosters is to him an ennobling and edifying work of art.

On the only other occasion when an architectural image is applied to his activities he has advanced far beyond the marking out of ground plans. 'This tymber is al redy up to frame' (III. 530), comments the narrator when the 'purveiaunce' has been completed for the climactic meeting of the lovers in the confidant's house. But, although the recurring image may suggest that he has persisted in his ideal of constructing a temple in honour of Love, other imagery already used of his conduct implies that it has been tainted by destructive and predatory attitudes of the kind that are characteristic of Diomede. The first metaphor to betray such an attitude comes very close indeed to that which is used of the Greek. Somewhat surprisingly it is spoken to Criseyde, suggesting to her that in attracting the love of Troilus she has made a 'good catch':

> ˙And right good thrifte, I prey to god, have ye,
> That han swich oon ykaught withoute net.'
> (II. 582–83)

When he has made arrangements for the meeting in Deiphebus's house, he urges Troilus:

> 'Lo, hold the at the triste cloos, and I
> Shal wel the deer unto thi bowe dryve.'
> (II. 1534–35)

When he enters his niece's bedchamber to prepare her for her lover's arrival, he conducts a campaign of mental and psychological attrition similar to that which Diomede will later prosecute; and he even employs the *blitzkrieg* tactics that earn the Greek the title of 'this sodeyne Diomede' (V. 1024). Although this epithet is never applied to Pandarus direct, it announces with threefold emphasis the result of his most effective stroke in the process of wooing. When Troilus, acting upon his friend's cue, enters Criseyde's room and throws himself upon his knees at her bed's head, Chaucer thus describes her astonished reaction:

> But, lord, so she wex *sodeynliche* reed!
> Ne, though men sholde smyten of hire heed,
> She myghte nat a word aright out brynge
> So *sodeynly*, for his *sodeyn* comynge.
> (III. 956–59 – my italics)

Pandarus surpasses Diomede in his deceitful words and contrivances, not only towards Criseyde, but also in his dealings with Deiphebus and other leading citizens of Troy. Moreover, if Diomede resembles 'hende Nicholas' in his direct approach to the lady, Pandarus resembles him in his ability to fabricate and execute ingenious charades in order to blear the public eye and bring the lady to bed. Nicholas's exploitation of the Mystery Play of Noah is hardly more fantastic — and more unscrupulous — than Pandarus's two productions that centre upon the invented figures of Polyphete and Horaste respectively.

One result of the intrusion of this ennobled descendant of the *fabliau* intriguer into the solemn scene of the consummation of a *fine amour* relationship is to produce something like the contrapuntal analysis of love achieved by Hugo von Hofmannsthal in his libretto for Richard Strauss's *Ariadne auf Naxos*. Here the librettist causes the barriers between the genres of *opera seria* and *opera buffa* to be broken down by contriving that an opera company and a harlequinade shall perform simultaneously their versions of the same love story — yet neither the poetry nor the music imply that the 'seria' element is in any way quixotic. Another result of the intrusion is that, by taking upon himself the baser, the less dignified and the more aggressive aspects of wooing, the confidant relieves the romantic lover of the need to reveal to his sovereign lady even the most tender of acquisitive impulses until the moment when he is able to declare:

> 'Now be ye kaught, now is ther but we tweye,
> Now yeldeth yow, for other bote is non.'
> (III. 1207—8)

Most lovers who adopt the converted Troilus's idealising attitude towards the beloved will thereby condemn themselves to serve her only at a distance: and many of them appear to be secretly content to do so — whether it leads them to a death-wish or to something like Pandarus's own 'joly wo' — because they are more in love with their own 'anima' (to adopt the terminology of Jungian psychology) than with the woman on to whom it is 'projected'. The prince is placed in the artificially privileged position of being served, not merely by an agent who procures him a mistress, but by a priest — almost a magician — who realises his devout fantasies for him by delivering an incarnate goddess into his embrace. But Troilus still has to pay a price, in terms of human relationships, for the privilege; and Chaucer shows us what the price is.

Although the ostensible function of Pandarus is to bring hero and heroine together, his perpetual presence succeeds only, at a profounder level of human intercourse, in keeping them apart. Indeed, the first complete scene in which the lovers appear alone together does not occur until Book IV and also happens to be their last appearance together in private. Moreover, it is the first time they see each other for what they are; and the result of this revealing interview is, ironically enough, their decision to separate temporarily on opposite sides of the military lines.

At their earlier meeting in Pandarus's house, Criseyde admits Troilus to her bedchamber only as a result of her uncle's fabrication about Horaste (the alleged object of Troilus's supposed jealousy), and so Troilus himself is obliged to make his entrance in the guise of jealous lover − a role which is totally alien to his nature.[26] When the youth faints (at the prospect of his lady's wrath at the very moment when he had expected to be admitted to the heaven of all his desires), Pandarus takes advantage of his conveniently silenced scruples and sensibility to lift him into the lady's bed and undress him 'to his bare sherte' (III. 1099). Even after that Pandarus remains, listening to the lovers' conversation, until he is satisfied that the spectre of Horaste − his own 'familiar' in one of its guises − has been finally laid. But, although the lovers are reconciled by the time Pandarus withdraws, the shadow of Horaste and the deceitful intrigue of Pandarus still lie between them, so Troilus remains in a false position − even though it allows him the somewhat masochistic satisfaction of being forgiven by his lady for a crime he did not commit.

At that moment, when they are at last left alone together, and left in this false relationship to each other, the narrative ceases, for the remainder of the scene, to follow any further the process of their mutual understanding − or lack of it. The only discoveries they continue to make about each other are physical and emotional as they consumate their love and the verse concentrates upon recapturing something of the rapture of that experience. The mode passes, as it were, from that of psychological drama to that of lyric opera.[27]

It is unfortunate that the term 'love-nest' has today become so debased; for this is precisely the image that Chaucer's verse applies to the *ménage* that Pandarus establishes for hero and heroine. Not only is Criseyde compared, in the most memorable simile in the poem, to 'the newe abaysed nyghtyngale' (III 1233−39),[28] but the establishment consists of security founded upon precariousness, permanent fidelity upon what is essentially a makeshift arrangement: the 'grete worthynesse' of love exists for the lovers 'bitwixen drede and sikerness' (III. 1315−16).[29] This can be seen from the way in which, as soon as Pandarus has withdrawn, the poetry reiterates the theme of present joy so lately come out of past sorrow; sweetness from bitterness. From the 'siknesse' of III. 1213 the verse advances to the 'sykernesse' into which Troilus is brought at III. 1243 − a condition that is anticipated in the preceding stanza in the 'siker' of III. 1237, where by deft metrical and syntactical placing, the word is made to stand out just as the nightingale's voice, to which it immediately refers, rings out. At the climax of the love-duet there is an almost Mozartian blend of smiles and tears in perfect equipoise as the lovers

   ... diden al hire myght, syn they were oon,
   For to recoveren blisse and ben at eise,

And passed wo with joie countrepeise.
>   (III. 1391–93 [1405–07])

Yet no sooner is equilibrium achieved than the scales are tipped in the opposite direction as Troilus experiences

> The blody teris from his herte melte,
> As he that nevere yit swich hevynesse
> Assayed hadde, out of so gret gladnesse.
>   (III. 1445–47)

The reason for this reversal is the advent of cock-crow, and the stern necessity of parting, which prompts the singing of the antiphonal *alba* that is set in motion by Criseyde's wishful, mythological fancy about Alcmena and Jove and concluded by Troilus's matching fancy about Apollo and Aurora.

The formality of the poetic writing establishes the text for the canon of a nocturnal rite that is celebrated at frequent intervals throughout the three years of the lovers' consummated relationship. Yet, at the same time, it emphasises the fact that what Pandarus has established for them is an arrangement whereby they meet exclusively for the purpose of celebrating the rites of Venus and Cupid. The poetry presents their relationship as essentially an aesthetic experience: they meet in order to rehearse a living work of art that is both beautiful in its human tenderness and sublime in its glimpses of the transcendental power of love. What they lack is the testing, diurnal experience of living together as man and wife, which demands other qualities besides aesthetic sensibility. For writers of romance – in any age – this would be of no importance. How important it is for Chaucer will be seen when we come to consider the debate between the lovers that concludes Book IV, where, apparently for the first time, Troilus comes up fully against the personality of the woman which the reader has been privileged to observe since the beginning of Book II.

PART TWO
THE ACTION

Chapter Four
The Fortunes of Love

Although the present study is concerned primarily with the human relationships in the poem, it is impossible to appreciate Chaucer's representation and analysis of them without also considering the role of the two principal personifications or daemonic powers who haunt the action. Something has been said already about the function of Cupid, but I have so far hardly mentioned Fortune, whose prominence in the story of Troilus is so marked that there are times when we are encouraged to wonder whether it is not the blind goddess, rather than Criseyde, who was the truly potent 'woman in his life'. Indeed, she appears to have usurped the heroine's rightful place in the poem's very first stanza. Whatever the reason for Chaucer's reticence about Criseyde (whether to shield or to slight her), the void created by her absence is filled by an allusion to Fortune when the poet promises to recount of Troilus 'In lovynge how his *aventures* fellen'. These are specified as his ascent 'Fro wo to wele' followed by his descent 'out of joie', a description which prefigures the schematic structure of the narrative's main action that consists of the 'comedye' (in the medieval sense) of Books I–III followed by the 'tragedye' of Books IV and V.[30] In so shaping the action of what is ultimately a 'tragedye' Chaucer has remoulded the 'matere' of *Il Filostrato* upon Fortune's wheel.

The impression that the narrative describes an arc of that wheel's revolution is enhanced by the balancing of details of the 'ascending' action against contrasted details of the 'descending' movement. Several of these carefully contrived correspondences have been noted by commentators.[31] What I would observe is that the impression of symmetry is achieved, not so much by the number, as by the variety of these parallels.

Correspondences may be extended: Diomede's wooing of Criseyde may be seen as an indecently accelerated travesty of Troilus's: both employ the diction of *fine amour;* but, whereas Troilus understands its phrases with a devout literalness, for Diomede they are little more than empty clichés that plot the milestones along the seducer's path into the lady's heart – or bed. Sometimes the correspondences are episodic: Troilus's visit to Criseyde's empty house (V. 519 ff.) is the counterpart to his triumphal processions past its windows in Book II; the letters whose texts are so painfully and painstakingly reproduced in Book V make a sad contrast to those exchanged in Book II; Troilus's dream

43

about Criseyde and the boar in Book V is the counterpart to Criseyde's about the eagle in Book II. Or a correspondence may be merely verbal: as Troilus's fortunes begin to mend, Chaucer says 'now of hope the kalendes bygynne' (II. 7); when he reads Criseyde's final letter, 'Hym thoughte it lik a kalendes of chaunge' (V. 1634) — where (as editors observe) there may be a play upon the idea of a 'kalends of exchange'. One of the subtlest is the double reference to the fall of Amphiorax — the significance of which has been discussed recently by Alice B. Miskimin.[32] Perhaps the most awesome is the contrast between the two public gatherings which flank the poem's central book. During the scene in Deiphebus's house Troilus, in order to be alone with Criseyde and their confidant for an hour, disposes of his favourite brother and Helen by asking them 'in a grisly wise' (II. 1700) to peruse a letter

> That Ector hadde hym sent to axen reed,
> If swych a man was worthi to ben ded.
>   (II. 1698–99)

— 'Woot I nat who', the narrator adds with studied unconcern. This subordination of the business of public justice to private ends, together with the callous attitude towards the hapless individual which is implied in the narrator's tone of voice, exacts its unwitting nemesis when, in the scene of the Trojan 'parlement', an issue of public concern ruthlessly, though unknowingly, decrees the permanent separation of the lovers.

The impression of symmetry that is produced by such correspondences causes the blind goddess to appear as a gigantic figure who holds in balance the two parts of the narrative like contrasted panels of a diptych, the one painted in bright colours, the other in sombre tones. Yet the impression that Fortune is the prime shaper of the action is a superficial one — in spite of the fact that it is several times entertained by the hero and encouraged by the narrator. Because it is superficial it is appropriate that it should be reflected in the poem's exterior structure. One purpose of the present study is, however, to show that there is a deeper and more organic process that is developed in counterpoint to the simple story of the hero's rising and falling 'aventures'.[33] This inner drama exists in the dialectic of human relationships. But, before we approach that inner drama, we should observe that Fortune is not even the more powerful of the daemonic forces; if any daemon presides over the action, it is the unfathomable god of love rather than the unpredictable goddess of luck.

Troilus first steps on to Fortune's deceptive escalator at I. 215:

> This Troilus is clomben on the staire,
> And litel weneth that he moot descenden;
> But al day faileth thing that fooles wenden.

But in the immediately preceding stanza we have been told that, angered by Troilus's hubristic taunts at lovers and their 'lewed observaunces',

> ... the god of love gan loken rowe
> Right for despit, and shop for to ben wroken.

Although Fortune is dignified with the title of 'executrice of wyerdes', carrying out (unwittingly) the administrative decrees of a higher power, her actions are in fact presented as the consequences of her merest whims. Cupid (as we have noted) is a more subtle daemon: the double turn in the hero's fortunes is engineered by this demi-god as a single pattern of nemesis. Moreover, the contrast between the panels of Fortune's diptych may remind the reader of that between the legends, in gold and black lettering respectively, that are inscribed above either side of the portal of the park to which Africanus leads the dreamer in *The Parlement of Foules* (120 ff.). The golden inscription declares the garden of love to be 'that blysful place / Of hertes hele', the realm of perpetual May that contains the 'welle of grace'. The black legend presents it as the haunt of Disdayn and Daunger; a sterile desert; and 'the sorweful were / There as the fish in prysoun is al drye' (138–39).[34] So nice is the balance between the blandishments of the one and the threats of the other that the dreamer stands motionless before the gates, like an iron bar caught between magnets of equal force (141–53). The allegory indicates how vulnerable to the vicissitudes of Fortune is the man who has committed himself to Cupid and his 'craft': for him, the partition that divides 'comedye' from 'tragedye' is slight indeed.

The most fatal shot fired in *Troilus* is the initial one which Cupid directs at the hero's heart, when he causes him to love Criseyde and to be incapable of ever loving anyone else. The simile of 'proude Bayard' (I. 218 ff.) illustrates the god's determination to bring Troilus under his discipline, even 'Though he a worthy kynges sone were' (I. 226). Indeed, Cupid displays a particularly cruel vindictiveness in causing a king's son to love a traitor's daughter during a war which — as Troilus is well aware (IV. 547 ff.) — was occasioned by 'ravysshyng of women'. The prince's remarks to Pandarus at IV. 547–60 imply that public opinion would never have tolerated the solemnisation of any liaison between himself and Criseyde; and we may be sure that public opinion would have been even more scandalised if it had known of the existence of such a liaison unsolemnised. The turn of events that interferes with the lovers' relationship at the beginning of Book IV is a cruel misfortune; but no great exertion on Fortune's part is required to realise what was potentially present in Criseyde's situation even before Cupid directed his arrow at the prince's heart.

It is true that, in both the 'ascending' and the 'descending' action, references to Fortune and the mutability of human affairs abound, but in each part there is only a single point where the blind goddess is represented as acting in a decisive and positive way. In the 'comedye' of

Books I–III the influential action that is attributed directly to her intervention consists of the rainstorm that detains Criseyde in her uncle's house overnight. The passage, clothed in grandiloquent rhetoric, has, gelded of its poetic inflexions, been cited as evidence of Chaucer's supposed belief in the absence of human free will: [35]

> But, O Fortune, executrice of wyerdes,
> O influences of thise hevenes hye,
> Soth is that, under god, ye ben oure hierdes,
> Though to us bestes ben the causes wrie.
> This mene I now, for she gan homward hye,
> But execut was al bisyde hire leve
> The goddes wil, for which she moste bleve.
>
> The bente moone with hire hornes pale,
> Saturne, and Jove in Cancro joyned were,
> That swych a reyn from hevene gan avale ...
> (III. 617–26)

Up to this point the deluge sounds as ominuous as that Virgilian storm which drove Dido and Aeneas into the cave and into each other's arms. But, in the lines that complete the second stanza, the merest suggestion of bathos is sufficient to deprive it of that formidable quality and to place it rather in the category of one of Rossini's repertorial thunderstorms that so conveniently assist the action in his operas — whether serious or comic:

> ... That swych a reyn from hevene gan avale,
> That *every maner womman* that was there
> Hadde of that *smoky* reyn *a veray* feere;
> At which Pandare tho lough, and seyde thenne:
> 'Now were it tyme a lady to gon henne!'
> (III. 626–30)

Moreover, Pandarus's Olympian laughter reminds us that the downpour was not exactly unexpected by him since, looking at the heavens with a meteorologist's expertise, he had chosen a time for his supper party

> Right sone upon the chaungynge of the moone,
> Whan lightles is the world a nyght or tweyne,
> And that the wolken shop hym for to reyne.
> (III. 549–51)

This stratagem is of the same order as Mrs. Bennett's, in *Pride and Prejudice,* who sends Jane to the Bingleys on horseback, instead of in the carriage, when a downpour seems imminent. Nor can the development in the weather have come as a total surprise to Criseyde, who had at first excused herself from accepting her uncle's invitation, protesting: 'It reyneth; lo, how sholde I gon?' (III. 562). On the further question of whether Troilus's presence in her uncle's house would come

46

as a surprise to her the poet is characteristically evasive, although he leaves little room for doubt about what she suspected (III. 568–81).

So the intervention of Fortune is not quite as decisive as it is declared to be. Indeed, as the intrigue of the 'comedye' moves towards its climax we are tempted to think of Pandarus almost as if he were the sole shaper of the lovers' destinies – an 'execut[or] of wyerdes' who possesses providential foreknowledge. This is suggested, for example, by the words that are used earlier to describe his final 'purveiaunce' for the assignation:

> For he, with gret deliberacioun,
> Hadde every thyng that therto myghte availle
> *Forncast, and put in execucioun* ... [36]
>
> (III. 519–21)

When, at III. 1667, the narrator announces the occasion for the next assignation, commenting 'for that fortune it wolde', we may feel that 'fortune' has become almost synonymous with 'Pandare'. It is therefore important to observe that Pandarus would shrink from making such a claim for himself; he is aware of his limitations and of the insidiousness of Fortune's conduct. When Troilus thanks him rather too effusively for having brought him into heaven, his friend hears him out 'sobrely' and then delivers three admonitory stanzas about 'fortunes sharp adversitee', recognising that 'wordly joie halt nat but by a wir' (III. 1618–38). Not that one should adopt an abjectly fatalistic attitude towards Fortune (as Troilus is prone to do); one must simply remember that 'nede is to werken with it softe'.

In keeping with this cautious respect for 'influences of thise hevenes hye' is the way in which Pandarus, before he sets out on his first purposeful visit to Criseyde at the beginning of Book II, 'caste and knew in good plite was the moone' (II. 74). His consultation of his *lunarium* does not imply that he was any more superstitious than most men of Chaucer's time; it indicates rather that, like most pragmatists and opportunists of any age, he believed that 'there is a tide in the affairs of men' and considered it prudent to consult the tide-tables in order to ensure that he had launched his 'grete emprise' upon a spring tide that would lead on to success.

Fortune's one, decisive intervention in the poem's second part is anticipated in the opening lines of the fourth and last of the formal prologues:

> But al to litel, weylawey the whyle,
> Lasteth swich joie, ythonked be Fortune.

In order properly to appreciate the force of this Prohemium to Book IV, it is first necessary to consider it in relation to its predecessors. One way in which Chaucer establishes the unity of the 'comedye' of his first three Books is by introducing a parallel, in terms of the religion of

Cupid, to the scheme of the three *cantiche* of Dante's *Commedia*.
Book I describes Troilus's apparently hopeless torment after his fatal
glimpse of Criseyde and begins, appropriately, with an invocation of the
fury 'Thesiphone' (I. 7–9). In Book II, though still suffering, he
becomes more hopeful, as if ascending the slopes of Purgatory. Indeed,
it may be significant that the first six lines of the book are an echo of
the opening of the *Purgatorio* (I. 1–3):

> Out of thise blake wawes for to saylle,
> O wynde, O wynde, the weder gynneth clere ...

In Book III he reaches Heaven with the consummation of his love. This
time the prologue consists of a hymn to a benevolent Venus (III. 1–49),
who is addressed as the power that knits the whole of creation together
in concord.

Few moments in the poem are more chilling than that, in the
concluding stanza of the fourth Prologue, when Thesiphone is again
invoked. We are thus reminded that the dismal Prologue to Book I was
not just the base-camp for the long ascent of the 'comedye', but the
prologue to the whole story of Troilus's 'double sorwe'. The atmosphere
is further darkened by the fact that Thesiphone is now accompanied by
her sisters who complete the trio of 'Herynes, Nyghtes doughtren thre';
and they are reinforced by 'cruel Mars' (IV. 22–25).

Nevertheless, as already noted, the power whom the narrator invokes
as supreme in the first stanza of this final Prologue is Fortune. The
moment of the downward turn in the action is the moment of the
goddess's greatest triumph. But, as in the account of her 'decisive'
intervention in the action of the 'comedye', the poet immediately sets
about the task of undermining her authority:

> And whan a wight is from hire whiel ythrowe,
> Than laugheth she, and maketh hym a mowe.

That final line of the stanza detracts from her stature by its
disrespectful anthropomorphism. Loss of dignity need not involve
diminution of power; but the second stanza, which specifies the actions
that are attributed to Fortune, may imply that her monopoly of power
is not as absolute as the narrator asserts:

> From Troilus she gan hire brighte face
> Awey to wrythe, and took of hym non heede,
> But caste hym clene oute of his lady grace,
> And on hire whiel she sette up Diomede.
> (IV. 8–11)

– which immediately suggests that IV. 2 might equally well read:
'ythonked be [Criseyde]'. And we are impelled to wonder whose
'brighte face' is turned away from Troilus. By the third stanza Criseyde
has become an acknowledged agent – though the poet does his best to

imply that she is a suffering and maligned agent. As the action of the book advances, so the arbitrary power of Fortune is discovered to be less supreme than the opening lines of the Prologue assert, whereas the element of human responsibility is seen to be greater than is allowed for in the standard medieval definition of tragedy.

This book — unlike its two immediate predecessors and, indeed, much of its successor — seems to adhere, both in outline and in detail, fairly closely to the text of *Il Filostrato*. The notable exception is Troilus's 'Boethian' soliloquy in the temple on divine foreknowledge and human free will (IV. 960–1078), in which the hero elaborates a sentiment that is entirely in conformity with the attitude towards human fate expressed in the Prologue's opening lines:

> 'For al that comth, comth by necessitee;
> Thus to be lorn, it is my destinee.'
> (IV. 958–59)

— Troilus complains. Partly because it is an obvious departure from Chaucer's principal source, this meditation has received much critical attention — a disproportionate amount, it seems to me. I do not mean to imply that the scrutiny is unjustified in itself; I merely regret that it has tended to distract attention from the rest of this crucial Book.[37] For the impression of the Book's close dependence on Boccaccio is a superficial one. Book IV is of central importance for an understanding of Chaucer's peculiar development of the action; both in its deepening awareness of the human predicament and in what it reveals of the true characters of the lovers.

The one event, affecting the lovers adversely, which is almost entirely attributable to Fortune, is that which is narrated immediately after the conclusion of the Prologue in which the wilful behaviour of the goddess is bewailed. It consists of the reversal on the battlefield that results in the capture of many notable Trojan warriors which, in turn, puts Calchas in the position of being able to negotiate the exchange of his daughter for Antenor. Throughout the poem Chaucer regards the battlefield as the place where Fortune operates in her most arbitrary fashion: battle appears like a game of 'hasard'. The movement of the whirligig of Fortune was graphically represented almost as soon as the narrative got under way:

> The thynges fallen, as they don of werre,
> Bitwixen hem of Troie and Grekes ofte;
> For som day boughten they of Troie it derre,
> And eft the Grekes founden no thing softe
> The folk of Troie; and thus Fortune on lofte
> And under eft gan hem to whielen bothe,
> Aftir hir cours, ay whil thei were wrothe.
> (I. 134–40)

The three stanzas that describe the death of Hector (V. 1541–61) are introduced by a reference to Fortune (who is here seen as the instrument of Jove's 'purveyaunce' and the partner of Fate). At the story's conclusion it is stated that, although Troilus and Diomede often met on the battlefield, 'Fortune it naught ne wolde, / Of otheres hond that eyther deyen sholde' (V. 1763–64) – though Troilus's death at the hands of Achilles is lamented in the words 'But, weilawey, save only goddes wille' (V. 1805).

The taking of the Trojan prisoners is as far as the arbitrary power of Fortune extends. At the hastily summoned 'parlement', Troilus deliberately forgoes an opportunity of attempting to prevent Criseyde's departure.[38] Nevertheless, it seems to him, after he has left the 'parlement', and especially in his meditation in the temple, that Fortune is responsible for his plight and that he is entirely at her mercy.

Soon after this occurs one of the most curious, yet one of the most significant, incidents in the poem: the episode of the tragedy that fails to take place. Although this passage follows Boccaccio fairly closely, its effect in the context Chaucer has provided is quite unlike that of the corresponding lines in *Il Filostrato*.

It is not until IV. 1121 that Troilus can bring himself to visit Criseyde. After only three stanzas of sorrowful, incoherent greeting, she is so overcome by emotion that she swoons (IV. 1149 ff.), and in the course of the next five stanzas Troilus is convinced that she is dead. His behaviour then becomes so theatrically ritualistic that he may seem to us almost a parody of the tragic hero. He formally lays out Criseyde's body for burial, and pulls out his sword in his determination to commit suicide so that his soul may follow hers even unto Hell:

> He gan hire lymes dresse in swich manere
> As men don hem that shul ben leyd on beere.
>
> And after this, with sterne and cruel herte,
> His swerd anon out of his shethe he twighte,
> Hym self to slen, how sore that hym smerte,
> So that his soule hire soule folwen myghte,
> Ther as the doom of Mynos wolde it dighte;
> Syn Love and cruel Fortune it ne wolde,
> That in this world he lenger lyven sholde.
>
> Than seyd he thus; fulfild of heigh desdayn:
> 'O cruel Jove, and thow Fortune adverse ...'
>   (IV. 1182–92)

– and he launches into an apostrophe which concludes with a formal leave-taking of his city, of the king his father and of his mother; he bids Atropos prepare his bier and beseeches Criseyde to receive his spirit. But at this point Criseyde revives and tragedy is averted. Her eyes 'glente / Asyde' and caught sight of his drawn sword. When she hears of his intended suicide she declares that, had that occurred, she would have slain herself 'with this selve swerd':

> 'I nolde a forlong wey on lyve han be
> After youre deth, to han ben crowned queene
> Of al the lond the sonne on shyneth sheene.'
>
> (IV. 1237–39)

So the story of Troilus and Criseyde might have ended like the tragedy of the 'star-crossed lovers', Romeo and Juliet — in certain respects the most 'medieval' of Shakespeare's tragedies.

Indeed, with Troilus's attribution of Criseyde's supposed death to 'cruel Fortune' and 'Fortune adverse', the episode envisages the possibility of the only kind of 'tragedye' that was customarily acknowledged by that name in the fourteenth century: it envisages a catastrophe in which the element of accident, deceptive appearances and arbitrary fortune would be maximal. As soon as the threatened catastrophe is averted, however, the situation to which the action reverts is seen to be, by contrast with this theatrically engineered episode, one in which there is far more scope for voluntary human action than Troilus had allowed in his perfunctory meditation in the temple.[39] Similarly, it is seen to be a situation where the arbitrary power of Fortune is far less supreme than the narrator had led us to believe in the Prologue.

It will be noticed that the occurrence that averts the 'tragedye' appears to be attributed to a higher power than Fortune. When Chaucer describes how Criseyde recovered consciousness in the nick of time, he remarks:

> *But as god wolde,* of swough therwith shabreyde,
> And gan to sike, and 'Troilus' she cride ...
>
> (IV. 1212–13)

Whether or not the italicised phrase amounts to anything more than a colloquial pleonasm is a question that will be discussed in another chapter. All that need concern us now is the situation the lovers find themselves in once the intruded calamity has been averted.

Even before the incident of Criseyde's swoon is narrated we learn that one positive course of action, that will enable the lovers to remain together, is open to them: Troilus can 'ravysshe' her — they can elope to a non-belligerent country. The most decisive act in the course of the 'tragedye' is the rejection of this plan in favour of the one proposed by Criseyde. This crucial decision is a voluntary act on the part of the lovers, although Troilus agrees to it very reluctantly. The adverse stroke of Fortune that decrees the proposed exchange of Criseyde for Antenor imposes the severest possible test upon the relationship between the lovers: until that moment it has blossomed and flourished in a secret garden; but now it can survive only if it is brought into the public eye.

The intrinsic inadequacy of the relationship to survive the challenge is painfully exposed during the debate that concludes Book IV.

Although the downward turn in the lovers' fortunes occurs at the beginning of this Book, the crux that determines the future of their relationship is contained within the disputation with which it ends. In the scheme of correspondences between the 'rising' and 'falling' action this contention is the discordant counterpart to the lyrical antiphony of the consummation scene in Book III. It is also the climax of a dialectical process that continues throughout the poem. This process involves not only immediate confrontations of the principal actors; it exists also in implied contrasts and conflicts between certain scenes and episodes, whether juxtaposed or remote. The remote contrasts consist not only of those correspondences between details of the 'ascending' and 'descending' action, of which something has already been said, but also of contrasted incidents within both the 'comedye' and the 'tragedye'.

Indeed, *Troilus and Criseyde* is nearly everywhere a markedly dialectical poem, in its incidental details as well as in its central issues. Not only are there scenes where one character exercises his powers of deliberative oratory upon another, but there are also soliloquies that discover a character formally debating with himself which course of action to adopt or what interpretation to put upon the experiences that have befallen him. It is in keeping with this dialectical spirit that, when Pandarus accuses himself of being a bawd, Troilus reassures him by employing a 'distinction' — 'Departe it so' — in the manner beloved of scholastic philosophers (III. 400–06); yet on another occasion Troilus himself complains of the academic ineptitude of Pandarus's attempts to console him with formal arguments.[40] In the scene of the Trojan 'parlement', a public debate is presented in counterpoint with a silent disputation within the hero's mind;[41] and, in an earlier scene, when Pandarus is deliberating with Troilus, he even imagines his friend's in turn imagining a contention within Criseyde's mind between two personified aspects of her being.[42] Even within a single speech or description Chaucer will take away with one hand what he has just given with the other; *contentio* is a prominent figure of speech; and we come to expect the solemn pronouncement of a *sentence* to provoke the tacit assertion of its contrary.[43]

Chapter Five
The Dialectic of Love – The 'Comedye'

(i) 'PEYNTED PROCES'

The dialectical process, which becomes most acute in the debate that concludes Book IV, is set in motion as soon as negotiations between the two parties to the love affair begin with Pandarus's visit to Criseyde's house at the opening of Book II. I have already discussed some implications of the architectural simile that the poet employs to commend the go-between's planning of his first diplomatic visit to his niece.[44] In fact, Chaucer's immediate source for the comparison is not a treatise by any follower of Vitruvius, but a text-book on literary composition: the *Nova Poetria* by Geoffrey of Vinsauf.[45] It is therefore not surprising to find that Pandarus's strategy exhibits the artfulness of one who is skilled in what the rhetoricians termed 'disposition'. This is to be seen particularly in his exploitation of techniques for 'amplification' of the kind that Geoffrey describes as *morae:* 'delays'. Delaying and allaying tactics abound in the confidant's devious approach to the disclosure of his business.

Indeed, he admits as much himself. When Criseyde, intrigued and exasperated by his continued prevarication, beseeches him to come to the point, he 'to coghe gan a lite',

> And seyde: 'nece, alwey, lo, to the laste;
> How so it be that som men hem delite
> With subtyl art hire tales for to endite,
> Yit for al that, in hire entencioun,
> Hire tale is al for some conclusion.
>
> 'And sithen thende is every tales strengthe,
> And this matere is so behovely,
> What sholde I peynte or drawen it on lengthe,
> To yow that ben my frend so feythfully?'
> (II. 255–63)

He adds in an aside:

> ... 'if I my tale endite
> Aught harde, or make a proces any whyle,
> She shal no savour han therin but lite,
> And trowe I wolde hire in my wil bigyle;
> For tendre wittes wenen al be wyle,

> Wher as thei kan nat pleynly understonde,
> Forthi hire wit to serven wol I fonde.'
>
> (II. 267—73)

When Criseyde, having at last discovered the true purpose of his visit, exclaims:

> 'Is al this peynted proces seyd, allas!
> Right for this *fyn*?'
>
> (II. 424—25)

she is, of course, seizing upon Pandarus's words '*thende* is every tales strengthe' and 'What sholde I peynte or drawen it on lengthe?' As for the term 'proces', which he employs here only in his aside, she derives that from his exclamation twenty-two lines further on, when he has still not come to the point: 'What sholde I lenger proces of it make?' (II. 292).

Even after he has resolved to come to the point, he continues in his 'fremde manere speche' for over a hundred lines until he at last announces the purpose of his visit at II. 316—20. Indeed, his flow of eloquence continues after he has imparted his news. It looks as though the concluding couplet of the revelatory stanza will constitute a perfect cadence:

> 'Lo, her is al. What sholde I moore seye?
> Do what yow list to make hym lyve or deye.'
>
> (II. 321—22)

But it is, in fact, only the spring-board for a new departure:

> 'But if ye late hym deye, I wol sterve, —
> Have here my trouthe, I nyl nat lyen, —
> Al sholde I with this knyf my throte kerve.'
>
> (II. 323—25)

Criseyde must not be allowed to interject before she has had time to absorb the shock and until an even more alarming prospect has been strategically set before her that makes the real 'aventure' appear mild by comparison. Whether he would kill himself we may take leave to doubt — though there can be no doubt about his genuine fear for Troilus's life (cf. I. 728).

In these aspects of his strategy Pandarus conducts his campaign in the manner of an advocate skilled in the techniques of deliberative and forensic rhetoric. But his talents go beyond that: he treats his 'grete emprise' as a living romance and regards himself as its author. He is disappointed to learn that the romance, with which the ladies are being entertained at the moment of his entry into the paved parlour, is not about love and that, consequently, there is no chance of its being exploited (like the story of Ceyx and Alcyone in *The Book of the Duchess*) as a stalking-horse under the cover of which he can creep allusively towards his goal. When his niece enthusiastically offers a summary of 'the story so far' he impatiently and condescendingly dismisses it:

> Quad Pandarus: 'al this knowe I my selve,
> And al thassege of Thebes, and the care;
> For herof ben ther maked bookes twelve ...'
>
> (II. 106–8)

He immediately sets about implanting in Criseyde a sense of curiosity and suspense with a skill that any writer of romance would envy. Finding himself in competition with such an epic as the Seven against Thebes, he fashions an epic style for his eulogy of Troilus as soldier and virtuous gentleman (which he manages to smuggle into the conversation in response to his niece's enquiry after Hector):

> 'Now her, now ther, he hunted hem so faste,
> Ther nas but Grekes blood; and Troilus,
> Now hym he hurte, and hym al down he caste;
> Ay wher he wente, it was arayed thus:
> He was hire deth, and sheld and lif for us ...'
>
> (II. 197–201)

Later, when Criseyde shows the first inclination to yield to Troilus's suit, her uncle adopts the style of a 'dream allegory' or 'love vision' in the tradition of Machaut. He seizes his opportunity when Criseyde enquires concerning Troilus:

> 'Kan he wel speke of love? ...'

adding, defensively:

> 'Tel me, for I the bet me shal purveye' (II. 504).

He responds by giving a very brief synopsis of his encounter with his friend 'this other day' (II. 554), concluding with an apology for not repeating all Troilus's words, since the emotional stress would cause him to swoon before her eyes (II. 574) – and, of course, because the reader has already heard them all in Book I. But the reader receives a bonus he had not bargained for: the synopsis is preceded by an account of (what is presumably) an entirely fictitious meeting between the two friends that antedated the one described in the earlier Book. Where Nature gave a leaden image, Pandarus returns a golden. He sets the scene for his romantic narrative beside a well in the palace garden where the two friends are engaged in manly, athletic pursuits. Eventually Troilus – with the improbability of a character in a dream allegory – expresses a desire to sleep and lies down upon the grass, while Pandarus continues to run up and down until he hears his friend groan. Then (just like the dreamer in *The Book of the Duchess*) he 'gan stalke hym softely byhynde' (II. 519) and overheard a petition to Love, lasting for three stanzas and couched in the devout terms of the religion of Cupid.[46] As well as suggesting the devoutness and purity of his love, this prayer is made to indicate Troilus's model discretion (II. 538–39), and so is Pandarus's account of his friend's reaction when he pretends to wake him (II. 551–53). Although this narrative may in some respects remind us of the innocent eavesdropping on the complaint of the Black Knight in *The Book of the Duchess,* the way in which it is employed to manoeuvre Criseyde into a receptive disposition towards the prince places it rather in the same category as Iago's recounting to Othello the fabricated tale about Cassio's calling out upon Desdemona in his sleep.

By the time Pandarus takes his leave (II. 596), he has convinced himself (though hardly the reader) that in her heart Criseyde really desires the liaison with his friend, even though she holds back from consenting to respond to his love with passionate love and merely offers 'love of frendes'. Her expressions of resistance to love are presumably attributed by Pandarus to that phenomenon known to medieval analysts of the female heart as Danger — the term applied to the sudden, irrational and inexplicable power of the lady to keep her lover at a distance or to 'cut him dead' just when the relationship appears to be advancing so promisingly. The direction of Pandarus's thoughts here is indicated in a later conversation with Troilus, where he imagines his friend in turn imagining a debate that is staged in Criseyde's mind between 'Kynde' who would pity his distress and 'Danger' who asserts:

'nay, thow shalt me nevere wynne' (II. 1376).

It is interesting to find Danger there opposed, not to something as superficial as Bialacouil, but to fundamental 'kynde' — Criseyde's 'real' nature.

In the *Roman de la Rose* Danger is personified as an uncouth villein who knows nothing of courtesy and with whom it is useless to parley. The only way to deal with him is to resort to trickery. This is precisely what Pandarus now feels entitled to do: in the various ruses that he henceforth practises upon his niece he is not deceiving 'the essential Criseyde'; he is merely trying to outwit her Danger. He is aware, however, that his niece is a sophisticated woman who knows all about contemporary theories concerning the psychology of love. As early as II. 384–85 he had pleaded:

'So lat youre daunger sucred ben a lite,
That of his deth ye be nat for to wite.'

Moreover, during their second interview he urges her not to play the tyrant any more, 'Al wolde ye the forme of daunger save' (II. 1243) — where the insinuation of the word 'forme' implies that, in his view, a woman's desire to preserve her 'danger' is indistinguishable from a wish merely to 'save face'. Nevertheless, although he may talk openly to his niece about her 'danger', this does not prevent him from plotting against it by stealth.

So far his stratagems have drawn upon his talents for inventing narrative fiction, whether in imitation of the romance, epic, or of the 'dream allegory'. But now he turns for inspiration to the drama, beginning with his arrangement for the 'accidental' passage past Criseyde's window of the mounted Troilus surrounded by his attendants. From this he advances to the enactment of true drama in the episodes concerning Polyphete and Horaste. The first of these productions is his masterpiece: only someone with a genius for intrigue would have thought of allaying all suspicion of the lovers' meeting by the bold device of inviting the whole of Trojan society to the trysting place! He rejoices in the opportunity for exercising his talents as actor-manager. He converts Deiphebus's house into a stage-set suitable for the performance of such a comedy as *The Alchemist* or *Le Marriage de Figaro*: a set that provides for the disposal of different groups of unwitting actors through conveniently positioned doors into various rooms, and into the garden, in such a way as to enable the private meeting to take place undisturbed. He has far more relish for this business than for the earlier negotiations with Criseyde, which involved him in such a protracted and sometimes precarious 'proces', soon discovered by his niece to be a 'peynted proces'. But as he narrates to the assembled company his fabricated story about Polyphete's supposed lawsuit against Criseyde's property, we find him involved in a 'proces' nearer his heart. It needs only a single line to give us complete confidence in his ability to hoodwink the Trojan notables: 'He rong hem out a *proces* like a belle' (II. 1615). Later a peal of metaphorical bells is characteristically imagined by Pandarus to celebrate his ultimate triumph: the moment when, Criseyde having at last accepted Troilus into her 'grace', the confidant falls upon his knees in his prayer of thanksgiving to Venus and Cupid (III. 183–89).

It is true that the love of Troilus and Criseyde has still to be consummated and that Pandarus plays an indispensable part in bringing this about; but what should have been his moment of supreme triumph is a little inglorious and, indeed, a little tarnished. For one thing, the theatrical quality of this second intrigue is somewhat inferior; partly because it re-employs devices already exploited in the affair at the house of Deiphebus. The setting up of the 'closed box' for the clandestine meeting is an altogether less skilful business on this occasion, involving the use of such crude stage properties as a secret passage and a trapdoor. The limitation of Pandarus's resourcefulness is also evident from his resurrection of the imaginary enemy: Polyphete being now metamorphosed into Horaste, who is hastily improvised when Pandarus discovers that, after all, the unpredictable Danger has a greater hold than he had imagined over his niece's 'hertes goost'. I have already emphasised some disturbing consequences of this fabrication;[47] others have yet to be observed.

(ii) RHETORIC INTO DIALECTIC

We do not have to wait, however, until the latter part of Book III in order to discover that Pandarus, far from being a vicarious author of the poem's plot, is as circumscribed as any of the other *dramatis personae.* In order to appreciate his human limitations and vulnerability it is necessary to look again, but from a different point of view, at the encounters with his niece that we have just considered. As he prepares himself for his visit, the date is the third of May, which several times in Chaucer's works has a certain ominous significance. For Pandarus it is an occasion when, 'for al his wise speche', he nevertheless 'Felte eke his parte of loves shotes keene' (II. 58). Denigrators of Troilus's manifestations of love as pusillanimous and paralysing must reckon with the way in which his friend here succumbs to a bout of green-sickness on account of feeling 'a teene / In Love'. After Pandarus has consulted his *lunarium,*[48] the poet, as a final piece of propitiatory 'purveyaunce' for his 'grete emprise', sends him on his way to Criseyde's house with the imprecation:

> 'Now Janus, god of entre, thow hym gyde!' (II. 77).

The purpose of this first interview is simply 'to get a foot in the door'; he would be unwise to exceed this self-imposed brief and to place himself beyond the protection of the demi-god invoked on his behalf.

In my earlier analysis of Pandarus's interviews with his niece I was concerned to abstract from the complex of Chaucer's narrative the scenario of the uncle's grand design, as he tried to act it out. But as soon as he crossed the threshold of Criseyde's palace, he had, in truth, passed over the frontier between rhetoric and dialectic. His carefully rehearsed performance is not permitted to remain behind a protective proscenium arch and work upon the feelings of an impressionable girl sitting passively in the auditorium. It is true that not all his questions are rhetorical; but Criseyde will not stick to the script he has imagined for her. His niece's interjections and counter-ploys tax keenly his powers of improvisation in the course of what becomes at times an almost desperate scramble on his part to reach the final curtain.

As elsewhere in Chaucer,[49] almost the first exchange is symptomatic of the situation that is to develop. For all Criseyde knows, when her uncle asks whether her book is about love, his enquiry may be quite innocent. After all, many men like to believe that young women beguile their time with stories about love when they cannot have the thing itself. How was he to know that the ladies were tackling anything as sombre as an historical *geste* (II. 83)? Indeed, Criseyde is at pains to explain that they are listening to no ordinary piece of romantic fiction: '*This* romance is of Thebes that we rede' (II. 100). However, her immediate reply to her uncle's enquiry teasingly pretends that he has some ulterior motive:

> 'Uncle', quod she, 'youre mistresse is nat here.' (II. 98).

The woman who can thus jest about non-existent ulterior intentions is likely to be shrewd enough to smell out those that are actually present. At II. 387 we find her doing just that. Having listened to Pandarus's protestations that he is asking her to offer Troilus nothing more than 'love of frendes' in exchange for his passionate service, she thinks to herself: 'I shal felen what he mene, ywis'. When she asks, with guileful innocence, what he would advise her to do, he falls immediately into the trap; he exceeds his self-imposed brief; places himself beyond the tutelary power of the 'god of entre' and urges her to return love for love.

Criseyde's bitter reaction to this proposal culminates in the stanza in which she denounces the 'peynted proces' with which her uncle has beguiled her. But there is one of his key terms that does not appear in her satirical anthology of his choicest phrases, because it had been singled out and disposed of in the preceding stanza of her speech. As we have remarked, on finding himself in competition with the momentous events of the 'romaunce' of the Seven against Thebes, he had employed his subtlest techniques of mystification and suspense in order to induce in his niece an irrepressible curiosity about the news he brings. He informs her that it concerns her intimately and he urges her to throw away her unflattering widow's habit:

> 'What list yow thus youre self to disfigure,
> Sith yow is tid so glad an *aventure*?'
>
> (II. 223–24)

And, as he approaches his climactic disclosure, he urges her to seize the proffered opportunity:

> 'For to every wight som goodly *aventure*
> Som tyme is shape, if he kan it receyven;
> And if that he wol take of it no cure,
> Whan that it cometh, but wilfully it weyven,
> Lo, neyther cas ne fortune hym deceyven,
> But ryght his owne slouthe and wrecchednesse;
> And swich a wight is for to blame, I gesse.
>
> 'Good *aventure,* O bele nece, have ye
> Ful lightly founden, and ye konne it take;
> And for the love of god, and ek of me,
> Cache it anon, lest *aventure* slake.
> What sholde I lenger proces of it make? ...'
>
> (II. 281–92)

Troilus had feared that Criseyde would be particularly resentful at such a suit when it comes from her own uncle (I. 1021–22); and his fears accurately predicted her first reaction: 'Is there no trust left in the world?', she asks, and points out to her uncle that if she had been so unlucky as to become infatuated with Hector, Achilles, or some other hero, it would have been his duty to reprove her without mercy or moderation. But it is the way in which she states this hypothetical disaster that concerns us:

> 'Allas! I wolde han trusted, douteles,
> That if that I thorugh my *disaventure*
> Hadde loved outher hym or Achilles,
> Ector, or any mannes creature ...'
> (II. 414—17)

If that would have been a 'disaventure', how can her uncle describe his information as 'goodly aventure' and 'good aventure'?

Criseyde has no taste for 'aventures' of any kind, unless they are safely enclosed between the covers of a book such as the Geste of Thebes. The only news that could give her any satisfaction would be the announcement that the Greeks had raised the siege (cf. II. 120—33); that would constitute the happy ending to the 'aventure' (which itself originated in an illegitimate love affair) that had bedevilled all their lives. The only previous occasion when she became personally involved in an 'aventure' was when her own father turned traitor and placed her in jeopardy. Ever since Hector championed her innocence her only ambition has been to achieve security in obscurity. The words 'siker' and 'sikernesse' continually reverberate in her mind when they are not actually on her lips. Anything that threatens to put this security at risk immediately alarms her. When Pandarus declares that he will kill himself on the spot if she does not offer some consolation to his friend, she does not pause to consider the likelihood of his executing this threat; the possibility of his creating a 'scene' in her house is enough to scare her into finding some way of humouring him:

> 'For myn estat lith in a jupartie,
> And ek myn emes lif is in balaunce ...'
> (II. 465—66)

It may be significant that she thinks of her 'estat' (468) before her uncle's life. 'Jupartie' (originally = 'a divided game; one where the odds are even'), like 'aventure', is a word that for her signals a menace rather than a challenge. Later in the Book, when she begins to entertain the idea of countenancing Troilus's love for her, she reflects:

> 'Sholde I now love, and putte in jupartie
> My sikernesse, and thrallen libertee?'
> (II. 772—73)

But, when Pandarus first informs her of Troilus's love and urges her to return it, he unwittingly unleashes a storm in her mind:

With this he stynte, and caste adown the hede;
And she began to breste a wepe anoon,
And seyde: 'allas! for wo why nere I deede?
For of this world the feyth is al agoon.
Allas! what sholden straunge to me doon,
Whan he that for my beste frende I wende,
Ret me to love, and sholde it me defende?'
(II. 407–13)

No sooner has she secured her way of life again after the consequences of her father's treachery have been faced than her closest remaining relative in the city, whom she thought her best friend, treacherously threatens to jeopardise it yet once more. Chaucer does his best to ensure that no reader misses the point that the woman, whom history represents as an archetype of treachery in love, rightly considers herself to be the victim of double treachery on the part of her 'nearest and dearest' at the very moment when she first hears of Troilus's suit.

Pandarus underestimates Criseyde's intelligence and takes little account of the effect that her predicament in Troy is likely to have exerted upon her attitude to 'aventures'. But, although his strategy fails to storm the citadel from without, he is helped by a partial capitulation from within: Criseyde is curious to know more about the prince who has been so affected by her beauty. Her uncle has good cause to smile (II. 505) when she asks whether Troilus can 'wel speke of love', even though (as we have seen) she claims that she requires this knowledge in order to rehearse her repertory of *ripostes*.[50] But the true advance in Criseyde's disposition to love occurs in his absence, when he has departed to plan with his friend the second phase of the wooing. The plan includes the arrangement whereby Troilus shall ride past his lady's house at a time when Pandarus has drawn her to the window – a stratagem which is duly put into execution at II. 1247 ff. But – with an irony that further detracts from his fancied role of omniscient author of a living romance – his stratagem is anticipated by the genuine accident of Troilus's riding past Criseyde's window on an earlier occasion when she stands there unprompted and alone (II. 610 ff.).

This genuinely accidental passage is better 'stage-managed' than that which Pandarus later contrives. Troilus is glimpsed by Criseyde as he returns in triumph from the battlefield, his horse wounded, his helmet hacked with twenty visible gashes and hanging from the back of his head by a 'tissue'; and his dented shield is stuck full of enemy arrows. This description of his heroic appearance is both preceded and followed by the enthusiastic plaudits of the crowd, to which he responds with a spontaneous and sober shamefacedness. These six stanzas frame the first idealised portrait of Troilus in the poem and, like the earlier portraits of Criseyde which we examined above, it endows its subject with something of a divine aura. Just as the 'hevenysshe, perfit creature' attracted Troilus

61

in the temple by what seemed to him a goddess-like disdain, so it is said of Troilus here that

> ... swich a knyghtly sighte, trewely,
> As was on hym, was nat, withouten faille,
> To loke on Mars, that god is of bataille ...
> (II. 628—30)

and,

> So fressh, so yong, so worthy semed he,
> It was an heven upon hym for to see.
> (II. 636—37)

And just as it was the transition from Criseyde's 'deignous' look to her lighter glance that moved Troilus, so it is his modest countenance, blushing for shame, with eyes downcast (cf. II. 645—48), that immediately moves the lady so that

> Criseyda gan al his chere aspien,
> And leet it so softe in hire herte synke,
> That to hire self she seyde: 'who yaf me drynke?'
> (II. 649—51)

One effect of the anticipation of Pandarus's scheme is to emphasise the innocence of the moment when the heroine is first moved by the sight of her unsuspecting lover and to preclude any doubt about the genuineness of the impulse that she feels. For, as the action advances, both hero and heroine, in different respects, become a little tainted by the ways of the world. We have seen how Troilus is compelled reluctantly to surrender something of his innocence in order to participate in his friend's stratagems. His second ride past Criseyde's window, though it can hardly be construed as a serious piece of duplicity against the girl, nevertheless constitutes his first act of complicity with Pandarus. The hero's contamination continues through his half-feigned sickness in Deiphebus's house to his counterfeit jealousy of 'Horaste'.

Although there can be no doubt about the sincerity of Criseyde's impulsive reaction to her first reported sight of Troilus, her behaviour is evidently meant to be contrasted with his at the moment when he first caught sight of her in the temple. He is there represented as the victim of fair and open warfare: he had provoked the god of love with his taunts, and the deity takes legitimate revenge upon him with a shot from his bow (I. 204—10). When the prince's confident glance penetrates the ranks of unimpressive beauties to be checked suddenly by the sight of Criseyde,

> 'O mercy, god!' thoughte he, 'wher hastow woned,
> That art so fair and goodly to devise?'
> (I. 276—77)

— as if he were in the position of a general who is forced to acknowledge that the enemy possesses a piece of very superior artillery that had entirely escaped the notice of his Intelligence Corps. Criseyde's response to her first sight of Troilus is quite different. Her exclamation, 'who yaf me drynke?' (II. 651) is usually interpreted as meaning: 'Who has administered a love potion to me?' Thus, even into the expression of this most spontaneous of all her responses is insinuated her half-conscious suspicion that she is being practised against by the most insidious of methods of moral assassination. After witnessing her uncle's performance, we can hardly wonder at her reaction. But, at the same time, we should not miss the point that, in spite of what she says, the potion is not administered altogether without her permission:

> Criseyde gan al his chere aspien,
> And *leet* it so softe in hire herte synke,
> *That* to hire self she seyde: 'who yaf me drynke?'
> (II. 649—51)

There follows one of Chaucer's more subtle pieces of calculated ineptitude. He makes the narrator intervene to defend her against the charge, on the part of 'som envious' detractor, that 'This was a sodeyn love ...' (II. 667): how could she have 'so lightly loved Troilus / Right for the firste syghte ...?' One commentator has observed that the result of the attempt to defend her is to implant in the reader's mind the very notion that the narrator is anxious to deny: 'This was a sodeyn love'.[51] That may be so. But, at the same time, the context of the tale itself, in spite of the teller's intervention, encourages us, as we have seen, to make an opposite judgement insofar as it insists upon our comparing Criseyde's reactions with those of Troilus at his first sight of her. The contrast is so pointed that the question of whether or not it is proper for a woman to react in the same way as a man at the first sight of the beloved is made to seem quite irrelevant. The word 'sodeynly' is applied twice (I. 274 and 306) and with propriety to the reactions of a man who undergoes a conversion as extreme as that which changed Saul into Paul and elicits from the delighted narrator the ejaculatory prayer:

> 'Blissed be love, that kan thus folk converte.' (I. 308)

On the other hand, in spite of her impulsive exclamation at II. 651 (which prompts the narrator's defence of her against the charge of 'sodeyn love'), it is not until II. 903 that Criseyde has even reached the point where 'she wax somwhat able to converte'. In defending her against the charge of sudden love, the narrator is made to commend her caution and wise circumspection. By this very act he disarmingly anticipates our suspicion, which increases as the account of her relationship with Troilus advances, that what we should perhaps be worrying about is rather the evidence of her tardiness and equivocation.

For the moment, however, she is genuinely perturbed and confused by contrary impulses. In order that we may be in no doubt about this, the poet internalises the dialectical process as she struggles with the problem of which course of action to adopt — 'That plited she ful ofte in many folde' (II. 697). Her agitated thought processes are not presented naturalistically, as in a novel, but are digested by Chaucer into a fairly formal interior debate: the arguments in favour of loving being presented first, accommodated into a stanza of *oratio obliqua.* This is followed by eight stanzas of direct monologue, which express the contrary view. These latter stanzas, like the opening stanza of *The Parlement of Foules,* see love at best as nothing more than a 'dredful joye'[52] and the whole discussion reveals Criseyde's preoccupation with her 'estat', her 'honour' and her 'name'. Such formalised treatment of the state of her mind certainly makes for compactness and lucidity, but there is a danger that it will give an impression of ratiocinative detachment. Chaucer, however, avoids giving such an impression, first of all by the memorable simile that dominates the stanza that effects the transition from the affirmative to the negative arguments:

> But right as whan the sonne shyneth brighte,
> In March, that chaungeth ofte tyme his face,
> And that a cloude is put with wynd to flighte,
> Which oversprat the sonne as for a space,
> A cloudy thought gan thorugh hire soule pace,
> That overspradde hire brighte thoughtes alle,
> So that for feere almost she gan to falle.
>
> (II. 764—70)

For a woman at such a moment reasons are the playthings of the emotional climate. It is interesting to see that, in the speech that is so introduced, Criseyde herself applies the same image to the condition of loving:

> 'For evere som mystrust, or nice strif,
> Ther is in love; som cloude is over that sonne.'
>
> (II. 780—81)

The other way in which Chaucer conveys a sense of her emotional fluctuation is by enclosing the debate between stanzas that declare that 'Now was hire herte warm, now was it colde' (II. 698). The second of these brings the scene to a conclusion with a climactic enactment of her vacillating thoughts:

> And after that, hire thought bygan to clere,
> And seide: 'he which that nothing undertaketh,
> No thyng acheveth, be hym looth or deere.'
> And with an other thought hire herte quaketh;
> Than slepeth hope, and after drede awaketh;
> Now hoot, how cold; but thus bitwixen tweye,
> She rist hire up, and wente hire for to pleye.
>
> (II. 806—12)

At this moment of indecision another external event, unplanned by Pandarus, intervenes to help to incline her towards love: namely, the singing by her niece, 'Antigone the shene', of 'a Troian songe' (II. 824–25).[53] All innocence, the young girl supplies the kind of vicarious artistic stimulus which Pandarus had hoped for from the romance to which the ladies were listening at the moment of his entrance, when he enquired: 'Is it of love?' Even the garden landscape in which the song is performed surpasses in romantic appeal that of the setting which Pandarus had imagined for Troilus's overheard declaration of love. The scene of the palace garden with its well (a conventional feature of the *locus amoenus* and of many a 'dream allegory') is far less distinctly realised than that of Criseyde's garden as it appears towards the end of the day:

> This yerd was large, and rayled alle thaleyes,
> And shadwed wel with blosmy bowes grene,
> And benched newe, and sonded alle the weyes,
> In which she walketh arm in arm bitwene ...
> (II. 820–23)

This is a rather more luxuriant version of Chaucer's own garden, described in *The Legend of Good Women,* where he falls into the sleep that brings his 'love vision':

> And in a lytel herber that I have,
> Ybenched newe with turves, fresshe ygrave,
> I bad men shulde me my couche make;
> For deynte of the newe someres sake,
> I bad hem strowe floures on my bed.
> (G-text, 97–101)

The song (after Machaut) proves to be, in fact, an unremarkable piece of romantic dogmatism, replete with commonplaces about the virtue of love. But it supplies the tonic that Criseyde needs after her reflections upon the stormy life of lovers, as it speaks of love for a knight who is, among other things, the 'stoon of sikernesse' (II. 843); and its conclusion in particular affords the reassurance that Criseyde requires in her present mood:

> 'Al dredde I first to love hym to bigynne,
> Now woot I wel, ther is no peril inne.'
> (II. 874–75)

Similarly, Antigone's biographical note on the poetess might have been calculated to give Criseyde what she wants to be told:

> 'Madame, iwys, the goodlieste mayde
> Of gret estat in al the town of Troye;
> And let hire lif in most honour and joye.'
> (II. 880–82)

Yet the most potent element in Antigone's performance is precisely the fact that it is not calculated, but completely ingenuous. There is mild irony in the way in which this inexperienced girl deplores (albeit in her song) those who

> 'Defamen love, as nothing of it knowe;
> Thei speken, but thei benten nevere his bowe.'
>   (II. 860—61)

There is deeper irony in the way in which the widow permits herself to be so impressed by the girl's confident effusions that she asks: 'lord, is ther swych blisse amonge / Thise loveres, as they konne faire endite?' (II. 885—86). But the schoolgirlish effusiveness of Antigone's response to this semi-rhetorical question is too patent for the older woman to ignore any longer. Chaucer captures vividly in the rhythms of his verse the girl's intonations:

> 'But wene ye that every wrecche woot
> The parfit blisse of love? why nay, iwys;
> They wenen al be love, if oon be hoot;
> Do wey, do wey, they woot no thyng of this!'
>   (II. 890—93)

So Criseyde abruptly changes the subject, observing: 'ywis, it wol be nyght as faste'. Nevertheless, the song has made its impression on her mind and helped her to be less fearful of love. It is at this point that we are told 'That she wax somwhat able to converte' (II. 903).

Although this statement may suggest a conscious decision on her part, much of the working of love upon her has been at a subconscious level; as is implied by the use of the verb 'synken' at II. 650 (upon her first sight of Troilus) and again here at II. 902; and more graphically by the image in II. 677 where it is stated that Troilus's 'manhod and his pyne / Made love withinne hire for to myne'. Having been permitted to eavesdrop upon her secret, but conscious thoughts, the reader is now privileged to enter into her subconscious and to perceive how it resolves the emotional disturbance for her during sleep. The nightingale who sings upon the cedar beneath her bedroom window 'Paraunter, in his briddes wise, a lay / Of love' sustains the romantic atmosphere as she falls asleep. But the bird's principal function is that it shall be metamorphosed into the white eagle of her dream, which tears her heart out of her breast and substitutes its own.[54] In her dream this aggressive act causes her neither fear nor pain. In other words: whatever protestations she may consciously make in her subsequent dealings with Pandarus and Troilus, she has already capitulated unconsciously. The aggressive aspect of love, which Criseyde unconsciously accepts, is something of which Antigone's song is altogether ignorant. But the dream does incorporate one feature of that song which we have not yet noticed: the theme of 'My true love hath my heart, and I have his'. The song's final stanza declares:

> 'But I with al myn herte ... wol love ...

My deere herte, and al myn owen knyght,
In which myn herte growen is so faste,
And his in me, that it shal evere laste.'
(II. 871—73)

Although in the dream the exchange is effected more violently, Criseyde experiences contentment with the bird's action as 'forth he fleigh, with herte left for herte' (II. 931). It is this longing for mutual love and trust, of which her life has been so far largely bereft, that affects her inclinations most profoundly.

That, then, is the extent to which Criseyde's mind has been undermined by love when Pandarus arrives for his second interview. He has already prepared Troilus for the part he must play: he first instructs him on how to deport himself as he rides past his lady's window (II. 1010—22) and then offers advice on the writing of a love letter (II. 1023—43). This is one of several places in the poem where the pedant in Pandarus is given full scope unwittingly to satirise himself: the academic character of the instruction is evident from the fact that it is almost entirely negative, consisting principally of a list of pitfalls to be avoided. But Troilus has no need of such commonplace advice: he has himself evidently studied the *Artes Dictaminis* and makes use of some of their more positive precepts. This can be seen from the list of appellations with which he greets his lady, as well as in the employment of *occupatio* and other unremarkable 'humility formulas' that succeed the opening address.[55] By adopting *oratio obliqua*, where *Il Filostrato* quotes the *ipsissima verba* at great length, Chaucer holds himself at an amused distance from the lover's efforts:

First he gan hire his righte lady calle,
His hertes lif, his lust, his sorwes leche,
His blisse, *and ek thise other termes alle,*
That in swich cas thise loveres alle seche ...
(II. 1065—68)

The acceptable clichés accumulate as Chaucer comments on them by implication through his incompetent rhymes and the calculated bathos of the concluding couplet:

And after that than gan he telle his wo;
But that was endeles, withouten ho;
And seyde, he wolde in trouth alwey hym holde;
And radde it over, and gan the lettre folde.
(II. 1082—85)

The narrator, however, loses patience with the 'humility formulas': when Troilus dutifully protests his worthlessness, he roundly comments that he 'leigh ful loude' (II. 1077).

Just as we have seen how revealing is a comparison of the account of

Troilus's first sight of Criseyde with that of her first sight of him, so it is instructive to compare with this letter the reply that Pandarus almost bullies her into composing with further threats of his friend's death, should she refuse to comply. As with the earlier letter, Chaucer merely supplies a summary, written in *oratio obliqua,* so that he may insinuate his attitude towards her performance into his recounting of it. The most obvious contrast lies in the fact that the reply is entirely innocent of the rhetorical formulas recommended by the *Artes Dictaminis.* This is perhaps to be expected from a woman who protests that this is the first letter she has ever written (II. 1213—14). On the other hand, in its unfumbling precision of expression it is a much more mature piece of epistolary writing than Troilus's — an impression which is enhanced by Chaucer's management of his stanza. When she sat down to write (we are told), 'she gan hire herte unfettre / Out of desdaynes prison but a lite' (II. 1216—17): the tight rein that she keeps upon her feelings is imaged in the control over diction and syntax:

> She thanked hym of al that he wel mente
> Towardes hire, but holden hym in honde
> She nolde nought, ne make hire selven bonde
> In love, but as his suster, hym to plese,
> She wolde ay fayn, to doon his herte an ese.
>
> She shette it, and to Pandare in gan goon ...
> (II. 1221—26)

Whereas Troilus's letter — even in summary — is diffuse (occupying three stanzas), this is almost ruthlessly compressed. The summary of his letter is paratactic, involving brief, detached clauses, end-stopped lines and some fumbling rhymes; the synopsis of Criseyde's is periodic in the all-embracing sweep of its carefully aimed trajectory whose progress is assisted by the continuous *enjambement.* And the bathetic effect of the final couplet of the stanzas devoted to Troilus is here avoided by the way in which the announcement of the folding of the paper — without any reading through of her manuscript — is postponed until the first line of the following stanza.

The artlessness of this letter is thrown into even sharper relief if we compare it with the text of her final missive to Troilus in Book V. On that occasion we are offered the text itself, complete and unedited. By abandoning *oratio obliqua,* the narrator seems to be abandoning responsibility for mediating the offensive contents of an epistle in which she dare not mention Diomede and cannot bring herself to state plainly that she will never return to Troy. Its hollow artificiality is evident from its first two lines, which have the air of being copied quite mechanically out of an *Ars Dictaminis,* or 'Complete Letter-Writer':

> 'Cupides sone, ensample of goodlihede,

O swerd of knyghthod, sours of gentilesse!'
(V. 1590–91)

We recognise at once the rubrics of a 'kalendes of chaunge' (cf. V. 1634). These are only the opening lines of an *exordium* that consists of an elaborately woven pattern of overlapping figures of speech that are too neatly turned to convey any genuine sentiment or carry any conviction:

'How myght a wight in torment and in drede,
And heleles, yow sende as yit gladnesse?
I herteles, I sik, I in distresse,
Syn ye with me, nor I with yow, may dele,
Yow neyther sende ich herte may nor hele.'
(V. 1592–96)

The internal rhyme, *myght / wight*, sounds glib; but the balancing of *heleles* against *herteles* as the second words of consecutive lines is more artful, especially when the association is clinched by bringing *herte* and *hele* together in the stanza's final line. The repetition of the first personal pronoun in the ante-penultimate, and the chiasmic patterning of the first and second person pronouns in the penultimate, lines add to the overall impression of over-written and artificial expression. In the main body of the epistle the colours of rhetoric give place, not unexpectedly, to the prevarications of hypocrisy.

But to return to the letter in hand. It is hardly surprising that when Troilus receives even this artless piece he is dismayed at the reply: it takes him a little time before 'somwhat he byheld / On which, *hym thoughte, he myghte* his herte reste (II. 1325–26)! The judicious restraint of this letter clearly falls short of what Pandarus had expected. Paradoxically, just because her heart is further engaged than he has guessed, she determines not to accede to his requests with the readiness he expects from her. When he had first produced Troilus's letter, she was both apprehensive and resentful, admonishing him: 'To myn estat have more rewarde, I preye, / Than to his lust' (II. 1133–34). Nevertheless, she takes the first opportunity of reading the letter in private, once it has been thrust upon her. She is evidently flattered by the epideictic flourishes and fumbling humility formulas (II. 1177–78).

The remainder of the stanza, that thus describes her reaction to the letter's contents, narrates what at first appears to be an altogether gratuitous incident. Criseyde, returning to the hall for dinner, discovers her uncle standing 'in a studye'. 'Or he was war' she playfully seizes him by the hood and declares: 'Ye were caught or that ye wiste'. This piece of by-play is her retaliation for his having forced Troilus's letter upon her by thrusting it into her bosom. It is clearly time for Pandarus to stop fencing with his niece. Having secured the exchange of letters, he feels able to make further arrangements without consulting her immediate wishes: her Danger must be overcome by his guile.

The sequence in Deiphebus's house, which constitutes Pandarus's greatest triumph, is preceded by two minor scenes of preparation that provide a timely comment on the go-between's moral stature. The first describes his visit to Deiphebus – a man in whose behaviour we see what was truly understood by the ideals of courtesy, *fraunchyse* and *largesse*. The fact that the go-between's stratagems require him to deceive such a generous and open-hearted person makes his devious conduct appear particularly obnoxious. In elaborating his rigmarole about his niece's supposed new danger, he adopts something like the 'fremde manere speche' (II. 248) with which he had earlier mystified Criseyde herself.[56] The prince's response unwittingly puts Pandarus in his place:

> ... 'O, is nat this,
> That thow spekest of to me thus straungely,
> Criseyde, my frend?'[57]

– a question which achieves the almost unparalleled result of reducing Pandarus to a monosyllabic reply: 'He seyde, "yis" '. Similarly, a comment upon Pandarus's lengthy 'processes' – whether 'peynted' or plain – and on all his cross-purposes and assays of bias is implied in the subsequent visit of Deiphebus to Criseyde while her uncle is present. The prince enters in the second line of a stanza and by its last line has taken his leave:

> And as thei casten what was best to doone,
> Deiphebus, of his owen courtesie,
> Com hire to preye, in his propre persone,
> To holde hym on the morwe compaignie
> At dyner, which she nolde nat denye,
> But goodly gan to his prayere obeye.
> He thonked hire, and wente upon his weye.
> (II. 1485–91)

(iii) THE THIRD ACTOR

An important technical advance in the history of Attic drama occurred when Sophocles introduced a third actor on to the stage. A similar advance appears in the two principal scenes of the central book of *Troilus,* where the relationships between all three grammatical 'persons' are brought visibly and tellingly into play. We have observed how Pandarus, insofar as he regarded himself as the only begetter of a living romance, was prepared to play all the parts; there are times when the lovers seem to him to be almost superfluous embarrassments. However, as soon as he crossed Criseyde's threshold, he found himself facing an antagonist, a second centre of consciousness. Nevertheless, he remains the protagonist throughout most of the scene of the declaration of love and for much of the scene that culminates in love's consummation. The fact that he remains indispensable in the very scenes where a third actor ought to be superfluous is (as already noted) in itself a significant comment on the relationship between the lovers.

In the scene of the declaration of love in Deiphebus's house the interplay between the three actors begins with two of them off-stage, while the third, imprisoned in his bed, overhears their mutterings but not the sense of what is uttered. To increase the suspense, the narrator intervenes to put a question to an apostrophised god of Love. This was the first time Troilus had ever declared his love to a lady: 'O myghty god, what shul he seye?' (II. 1757). And with that query the author closes the book.

The action remains suspended for the first fifty lines of Book III while the poet sings his hymn to Venus. When the curtain rises again Troilus is discovered still alone in bed, his mind preoccupied with the question that closed the previous book. Whereas Pandarus seems to have developed the strategy for his first visit to Criseyde from a study of the principles of rhetorical *dispositio*, Troilus has undoubtedly prepared himself for his first interview with her by studying all the other four Parts of Rhetoric, though at a very elementary level. He has evidently paid attention (though never so briefly) to *Inventio* – 'Thus wol I pleyne unto my lady dere'; *Elocutio* – 'That word is good'; *Pronunciatio* – 'This shal be my cheere'; and *Memoria* – 'Thys nyl I nat foryeten in no wise' (III. 50–55)! Of these only the last two require any comment. The art of *Pronunciatio* included, not only oral delivery, but the suiting of the action to the word – either the appropriate accompanying gesture or apt facial expression. It will be recalled how the knight in *The Squire's Tale,* who presents the horse of brass and who rivals even Gawain in the 'teccheles termes of talkyng noble',[58] addresses the company with faultless rhetoric:

> And, for his tale sholde seme the bettre,
> Accordant to his wordes was his cheere,
> As techeth art of speche hem that it leere.[59]
>
> (*CT*. F. 102–4)

Fortunately for the reader, as well as for the ingenuousness of Troilus's plea to his lady, the techniques for *Memoria* fail him. Had he not forgotten his recorded lesson (III. 51) in epideictic oratory ('to preysen hire' [III. 84]), we might have been treated to an exhibition equivalent to the exercise in the *Artes Dictaminis* that constituted his first letter to the girl.[60]

Before he recovers himself sufficiently to express his feelings in a coherent manner, Criseyde has spoken to him. Her opening remark would hardly qualify for inclusion in an anthology of 'Memorable First Utterances of the World's Great Lovers'. In reply to Troilus's feebly groping question, 'Who is al there? I se nought, trewely', she informs him precisely: 'Sire ... it is Pandare and I' (III. 68). While the dazed and dazzled Troilus is expecting an epiphany of his goddess through the bed-curtains, we are presented with this very factual woman. Her reply is not merely prosaic: it is defensive; Criseyde will not detach herself, even verbally, from her kinsman. She continues for some time in this manner that is both guarded and brisk. When Troilus would rise from his bed to kneel in homage to her, as a lover should kneel before his sovereign lady, she restrains him gently with both hands and deliberately misunderstands his intentions. She persists in acting out the public reason for her visit: it is she who should be kneeling to him — she protests — in order to thank him for his protection in the matter of Polyphete. The business-like attitude shapes her sentences:

> 'Sire, comen am I to yow for causes tweye:
> First yow to thonke, and of youre lordshipe eke
> Continuance I wolde yow biseke.'
>
> (III. 75—77)

The doctrinaire lover, finding the expected roles reversed on hearing 'his lady preye / Of lordshipe hym', is so embarrassed that he forgets his conned speech. But the rhetoric of the heart supplants that of the 'arts of speech' and he pronounces a 'pleynte' that is as moving as its syntax is unsophisticated and its sentiments commonplace (III. 98—112). The new dispensation even supplies him with the appropriate 'cheere' for the delivery of his speech, as we have already observed.[61]

Although Criseyde is continually exhorted and nudged by Pandarus — and even mimicked by him in exasperation (III. 121—22) — she will not be hustled. Another, longer, more impassioned, but no less simple, plea (III. 127—46) is required from Troilus before she will accept him into her 'service'. In spite of her refusal to be hurried by her uncle, she continues to exploit the presence of a third actor, using Pandarus less as a refuge now and more as a stalking-horse. After Troilus's first plea she speaks about him in the third person to her uncle: 'I wolde hym preye / To telle me the fyn of his entente' (III. 124—25). Even after his second plea she persists in talking across her lover in this way until the last line of her first complete stanza: 'Now beth al hool, no lenger ye ne pleyne' (III. 168). But, at the beginning of the next stanza, the brake is immediately applied again with her warning against his refusing her woman's privilege of sovereignty in such a relationship. In her final stanza the rhythms are relaxed as the emotional temperature is allowed to rise until, within the concluding couplet, words issue in unexpected action:

> 'For every wo ye shal recovere a blisse';
> An hym in armes took, and gan hym kisse.
>
> (III. 181—82)

Her control of the situation is indicated not only in the movement of her speech, but in the organisation of its syntax. As with her untutored letter to Troilus in Book II, her sophisticated nature is revealed by her apparently instinctive use of periodic sentence structure. She even manages to shape one pointed admonishment as a chiasmus: 'As I wel mene, ek mene wel to me' (III. 164). But her most telling piece of syntactic manipulation occurs at the very opening of the speech (III. 159), where the succinct proviso 'Myn honour sauf' is suspended, as an absolute construction, above all that follows. It not only places a restraining hand upon the too readily yielding 'I wol wel trewely' that completes the line, but makes its presence uncomfortably felt throughout the whole of the periodic sentence which is not completed until the end of the next stanza at the miraculous moment when she abandons the Third Person, along with the third actor, to address her lover exclusively and direct.

In the consummation scene, later in the Book, the deployment of the three actors and the play of perspective lighting are handled with particular subtlety in the brief episode that follows the entrance of Troilus, the last of the three to appear. We have already encountered several striking examples of the way in which a new episode is pointedly contrasted with an earlier one; not only as between various scenes that help to underline the partial symmetry of the 'ascending' and 'descending' action, but also between such episodes as the lovers' separate first glimpses of each other, their respective epistles, and the two 'progresses' of Troilus past Criseyde's window. In these episodes the correspondences, though extremely significant, are usually implicit. But, as a result of close verbal parallels, the entrance of Troilus to the other two actors here is explicitly contrasted with their entrance to him, as he lay in his feigned sick-bed, at the beginning of Book III. Now it is Criseyde who lies in bed and, as she catches sight of her 'servant' kneeling 'by hire beddes heed', Chaucer describes her reaction in words I have already quoted to illustrate Pandarus's employment of the surprise attack, in the manner of 'this sodeyn Diomede', as he directs Troilus's operations:

> But, lord, so she wex sodeynliche reed!
> Ne, though men sholde smyten of hire heed,
> She myghte nat a word aright out brynge
> So sodeynly, for his sodeyn comynge.
> 　　　　　　　(III. 956–59)

At this point in the linear action, however, reader and actors alike are still happily ignorant of Diomede and his ways: the reader is in fact being referred back to the account of Troilus's discomfiture in the earlier scene that causes him to forget his prepared address of love:

> This Troilus, that herde his lady preye
> Of lordshipe hym, wex neither quyk ne dede,
> Ne myghte o word for shame to it seye,
> Although men sholde smyten of his hede;
> But, lord, so he wex sodeynliche rede ...
> 　　　　　　　(II. 78–82)

One of the ways in which Chaucer demonstrated, in the earlier scene, that

Criseyde was mistress of the situation was in making her restrain Troilus
by laying her 'hondes softe' upon him as he attempted to raise himself
from his sick-bed in order to do homage to her. A measure of the changed
situation in the later scene is that he now succeeds immediately in kneeling
beside her bed and she is so confused that she fails to ask him to rise from
this posture, as fourteenth-century etiquette demanded (III. 967 ff.).

It is this situation which prompts Pandarus to run for the cushion for
his friend to kneel upon — an action for which he has been much mocked
and maligned. C. S. Lewis has aptly remarked that if we suppose he does it
as a joke, his action 'is hardly funny at all, it is merely silly'.[62] Lewis sees
it as an example of the fact that, although Pandarus is no busybody, he
nevertheless 'has the fussiness of the busybody; even when there is nothing
to be done, he must needs do something'.[63] But it seems to me that the
situation is one where something desperately needs to be done and
Pandarus knows just what to do.[64] Chaucer writes:

> But Pandarus, that so wel koude feele
> In every thyng, to pleye anon bigan,
> And seyde: 'nece, se how this lord kan knele!
> Now, for youre trouthe, se this gentil man! [']
> And with that word he for a quysshen ran,
> And seyde: 'kneleth now, whil that yow leste,
> Ther god youre hertes brynge soone at reste!'
> (III. 960–66)

An ability to 'fele' — to probe a situation, to sense an atmosphere — is
certainly needed. Criseyde has been reduced to speechlessness by Troilus's
sudden appearance and he is too ashamed to speak, on account of the
uncongenial role of jealous lover that has been foisted upon him.
Something is needed to break the tense atmosphere that Pandarus is
himself partly responsible for creating; so he 'to pleye anon bigan'. But the
'pleye' does not consist exclusively in the act of running for the hassock:
the speech that surrounds the action is just as important. He appeals to
Criseyde's delicate sense of social propriety, so forcibly expressed in the
earlier scene when one from whom she sought 'continuance' of 'lordshipe'
attempted to kneel in homage before her:[65] 'se how this *lord kan
knele*!', he exclaims. When she fails to ask Troilus to rise, Pandarus runs
for the cushion as if to say to him: 'It seems you will have to kneel there
all night, so you may as well be comfortable while you are about it!'.

That this is the correct interpretation is confirmed by the next stanza,
in which the narrator pretends to search for some adequate reason to
explain why 'she bad hym nat rise':

> If sorwe it putte out of hire remembraunce,
> Or elles that she took it in the wise
> Of dewete, as for his observaunce ...
> (III. 968–70)

Failing to find an answer, he quickly turns to the positive outcome of Pandarus's piece of psychological 'pleye':

> But wel fynde I she dede hym this plesaunce,
> That she hym kiste, although she siked sore,
> And bade hym sitte adown withouten more.
>
> (III. 971–73)

With the success of this little stratagem, Pandarus judges that he can now withdraw as far as his first line of retreat (romance reading by the fireside), though he has to rush into the front line once more (at III. 1190) to rescue his unconscious friend before he feels that he can finally leave him to make his own way to the heaven of Cupid.

During the lovers' three year sojourn in that heaven, dialectic is softened into antiphony; but, eventually, the searching dialectical 'process' is set in motion again and impels Troilus's fortunes towards the ultimate 'tragedye'.

Chapter Six
The Dialectic of Love – The 'Tragedye'

(i) PANDARUS ECLIPSED

Like its predecessor, Book IV culminates in a long scene with the lovers in bed. But now all is changed:

> Whan they were in hire bed in armes folde,
> Naught was it lik the nyghtes here byforn;
> For pitously ech other gan byholde,
> As they that hadden al hire blisse ylorn,
> Bywaylinge ay the day that they were born.
>
> (IV. 1247–51)

In the earlier scene the genial spirit of Pandarus hovered benignly about them, performing his priest-like ministrations before he gradually and discreetly withdrew to allow them to enter into the oblivion of love's intimate heaven. But in the later scene he has departed even before Troilus arrives. The lovers are left to contemplate the dismal situation unsupported; but more important is the fact that they are left to face each other alone and are no longer allowed to escape into erotic oblivion.

The abdication of Pandarus from his sacerdotal role begins, in fact, much earlier in Book IV. Indeed, to some readers it may seem to be complete by IV. 401–03, when he tries to console his friend by reminding him that 'This town is ful of ladyes al aboute' who, in his judgement, are 'fairer than swiche twelve / As evere she was'. At first this advice may seem as grating and as insensitive as the duck's contribution to the solution of the hard *demande d'amour* posed in *The Parlement of Foules*: 'There been mo sterres, Got wot, than a payre' (595). We may feel moved to borrow from the 'gentil tercelet' the phrases in which he scorns this uncourtly attitude, and apply them to Pandarus:

> 'Thou farest by love as oules don by lyght:
> The day hem blent, ful wel they see by nyght.
> Thy kynde is of so low a wrechednesse
> That what love is, thow canst nat seen ne gesse.'
>
> (*ibid*. 599–602)

A more careful reading of the episode will, however, show that such an accusation is altogether misplaced. When, in the corresponding passage in *Il Filostrato*, Pandaro offers Troilo similar advice, it is indeed to be taken at its face value. But in Chaucer's handling of the episode – which, superficially viewed, depends very closely on Boccaccio – nothing is so straightforward; everything proceeds by way of implication, slightly ambiguous motivation and lucky improvisation. What the scene does reveal about Pandarus is that the resourcefulness of this capable minister is hard pressed to match the requirements of the new situation.

When he entered Troilus's guarded chamber he was, most uncharacteristically, 'So confus, that he nyste what to seye; / For verray wo his wit was neigh aweye' (IV. 356–57). His arguments are hastily improvised mainly in order to establish contact with his semi-conscious friend and to engage his mind in some kind of reasoned discourse. He seems to recognise instinctively that, the more outrageous his utterances, the more effective they will be. His advice that Troilus should seek consolation in the arms of another lady does not sound very genuine when spoken by a lover who, in the immediately preceding stanza, has pointedly drawn attention to his own plight as a faithful, but unrequited, 'servant'. Moreover, even the consolation offered in that stanza was no less disingenuous: Troilus is not entitled to complain, 'Syn thi desir al holly hastow had' (IV. 395). It is rather he, Pandarus, who should weep, because he has 'nevere felte in my servyse / A frendly cheere, or lokyng of an eye' (IV. 396–97). This sentiment flatly contradicts his memorable warning to his friend at III. 1625:

> 'For of Fortunes sharp adversitee
> The worste kynde of infortune is this:
> A man to han ben in prosperitee,
> And it remembren whan it passed is.'

The contradiction is sharply pointed out by Troilus at IV. 477–83. Just in case the reader has failed to take the point about Pandarus's desperate tactics in recommending other ladies to his friend, the narrator underlines it for him:

> Thise wordes seyde he *for the nones* alle,
> To helpe his frend, lest he for sorwe deyde;
> For douteles *to don his wo to falle*
> *He roughte nat what unthrift that he seyde.*
> (IV. 428–31)

A reader who is well able 'it remembren whan it passed is', and who has a sensitive ear for verbal echoes, may experience here a decided sense of *déjà entendu.* At his very first entry in Book I Pandarus had employed a similar psychological subterfuge to rouse his prostrate friend, taunting him with the accusation that fear has driven him into a fit of religious melancholy. The narrator's interjection begins with the very words that introduce his comment in Book IV, but he makes his point more explicitly:

> Thise wordes seyde he for the nones alle,
> That with swich thing he myght him angy maken,

> And with an angre don his sorwe falle,
> As for the tyme, and his corage awaken;
> But wel wist he, as fer as tonges spaken,
> Ther nas a man of gretter hardinesse
> Than he, ne more desired worthinesse.
>
> (I. 561—67)

The fact that he is obliged to snatch, in his confusion, at this already used tactic suggests how limited his resources are.[66] Nevertheless it works, in spite of the fact that when the performance first reaches Troilus: 'Oon ere it herde, at tother out it wente' (IV. 434). Troilus's sense of the falsity and outrageousness of Pandarus's arguments increases as he disposes of them in turn. Eventually he explodes in scornful indignation:

> 'But kanstow pleyen raket to and fro,
> Netle in, dokke out, now this, now that, Pandare?'
>
> (IV. 460—61)

The 'ding-dong' rhythm and the 'ping-pong' imagery vividly convey Troilus's sharp caricature of Pandarus's prevarications. The expostulation reaches its climax in an inquisitorial battery directed mercilessly against the exposed Second Person pronoun:

> 'But telle me this, syn that *the* thynketh so light
> To chaungen so in love, ay to and fro,
> Whi has*tow* nat don bisily *thi* myght
> To chaungen hire that doth *the* al *thi* wo?
> Whi nyl*tow* love an other lady swete,
> That may *thyn* herte setten in quiete?'
>
> (IV. 484—90)

This is followed through by the taunt — particularly galling to Pandarus, the man of the world — that he argues like an academic immured in an ivory tower:

> 'O, where hastow ben so longe in muwe,
> That kanst so wel and formaly arguwe?'
>
> (IV. 496—97)

The effect of this retort is, for the first time in the poem, to reduce Pandarus to silence (IV. 521—22); an adumbration of the silence into which he finally lapses at V. 1723—29. He realises that his attempt to ward off his friend's thoughts of suicidal despair by keeping his mind engaged in debate cannot be sustained any longer; some more substantial means of consolation must be found before he loses the attention of Troilus which he has taken such pains to acquire. So he proposes the abduction of Criseyde; only to discover that he has been anticipated by Troilus, who has, moreover, also considered the objections to such a measure. But now that a practical course of action is envisaged Pandarus recovers something of his former confidence: he is prepared to risk his life in his friend's service, and is able to persuade him to allow him to arrange a meeting with his lady to see if she will consent to the plan.

Before the arrival of Pandarus at her palace, Criseyde receives two less welcome visits. The first is from personified Fame — who brings the rumour of the 'parlement's' decision. Then Criseyde's uncertainty about what she has overheard is unpleasantly resolved by the visit of the Trojan gossips, who provide an interlude of bitterly ironical comedy which in fact contains more of Boccaccio than of Chaucer. After their departure, she is vouchsafed the equivalent of an operatic *scena* — a formal soliloquy which the narrator afterwards refers to as 'Hire heigh compleynte' as he cuts it short with a characteristic 'inexpressibility *topos*'. The contrived intervention of the narrator here is one of the most ironical of Chaucer's stratagems in the poem:

> How myghte it evere yred ben or ysonge,
> The pleynte that she made in hire destresse?
> I not; but, as for me, my litel tonge,
> If I discryven wolde hire hevynesse,
> It sholde make hire sorwe seme lesse
> Than that it was, and childisshly deface
> Hire heigh compleynte, and therfore ich it pace.

(IV. 799—805)

But his tongue has already proved to be too large and has defaced the 'heigh compleynte' by childishly blurting out truths about Criseyde's feelings and motives that an uncritical encomiast would have eschewed.

It is Criseyde's 'tonge' rather than the narrator's that has proved to be too 'litel'. She is endowed with a voice that enables her to bear admirably her part in an *aubade,* but she has neither the *tessitura* nor the weight of the dramatic soprano for whom high complaints are composed. Finding herself suddenly in the position of a tragic heroine, she tries bravely to live up to the role. She rends her hair, wrings her fingers and beats her breast as she calls upon death and regrets, not only that she had even seen Troilus, but that she had ever been born 'in corsed constellacioun'. She believes she must die since, being deprived of Troilus, she lacks her 'kynde noriture' (IV. 768) and so must wither like a rootless plant. But gradually, from the beginning of the following stanza, the familiar 'wys' Criseyde begins to assert herself again until she has entirely superseded the tragedy queen.

It may be this sense of being deprived of her 'kynde noriture' that decides her in favour of a passive course of starvation rather than one of actively seeking a more violent death; in any case she dare not handle weapons 'for the crueltee' (IV. 772). In the course of the next stanza the contemplated moment of death seems to be receding rapidly into a vague future. She assures an apostrophised Troilus that she will wear black 'in tokenyng ... / That I am *as* out of this world agon' (IV. 779—80). It seems that her intentions have now substituted for actual death the metaphorical 'death to the world' symbolised by the outwardly black habit of a nun.[67]

She even prescribes a religious 'rule' for herself:

> 'And of myn ordre, *ay til deth me mete,*
> The observaunce evere, in youre absence,
> Shal sorwe ben, compleynte, and abstinence.'
> (IV. 782—84)

That meeting no longer seems to be so imminent and, in any case, it is up to Death to take the initiative now that she has laid the responsibility at his door by abandoning any serious intention of suicide. Having postponed the bitter realities of death to such a safe distance, she can afford to indulge in some romantic, mythological fancies about her life with Troilus in the next world. The neat turns of rhetoric, in the third and fourth lines quoted below, help to turn all to favour and to prettiness:

> 'Myn herte, and ek the woful goost therinne,
> Byquethe I with youre spirit to compleyne
> Eternaly, for they shul nevere twynne;
> For though in erthe ytwynned be we tweyne,
> Yit in the feld of pite, out of peyne,
> That hight Elisos, shal we be yfeere,
> As Orpheus with Erudice his fere.'
> (IV. 785—91)[68]

In the concluding stanza of her complaint she considers Troilus's reactions to the situation:

> 'But how shul ye don in this sorwful cas,
> How shal youre tendre herte this sustene?
> So ye wel fare, I recche nat to deye.'
> (IV. 794—98)

Her altruism is undoubtedly genuine; but her expression of anxiety concerning how Troilus's 'tendre herte' will be able to sustain the turn of events carries with it the insidious suggestion that her own heart may not find the weight of sorrow altogether insupportable. The stanza also confirms Criseyde in her unquestioning acceptance of the situation with which fate has presented her: 'Thus, herte myn', she says in her apostrophe to Troilus, 'for Antenor, allas, / I soone shal be chaunged, as I wene'; and, completely resigned to this fate, she urges him to 'foryete this sorwe and tene / And me also'. An ironical counter-melody that fits these verses may steal into the mind of the knowing reader: 'Thus, herte myn, for *Diomede,* allas, / *Ye* soone shal be chaunged' ... 'and *I* shal foryete this sorwe and tene, / And *yow* also'! Her resignation is so complete that she never entertains the thought that she, or anyone else, might take some initiative to prevent the exchange from being brought about. And it is at this moment that Pandarus arrives with Troilus's proposal that she should take just such an initiative.

The alarming feature of their interview is that the resourceful executive, who had become almost a personification of benevolent fortune, resigns to Criseyde his role of supreme strategist. The resources that sustained his prolonged and devious arguments during his first interview in Book II are depleted; by comparison he is almost perfunctory. He is now a mere messenger rather than self-appointed plenipotentiary:

> 'This, short and pleyn, theffect of my message,
> As ferforth as my wit kan comprehende;
> For ye, that ben of torment in swich rage,
> May to no long prologe as now entende ...'
> (IV. 890–93)

Since his wit is failing, he urges: 'And lat sen how *youre* wit shal now availle' (IV. 937) – and adds the rather feebly chiming assurance: 'And that that I may helpe, it shal nat faille'. He has rationalised his abdication of initiative to the girl by appealing to the authority of one of the more doubtful generalisations from his stock of maxims: 'Wommen ben wise in short ayvsement'. So he leaves it to her to find some way with Troilus to 'destourbe youre goynge'. In urging this he is merely conveying Troilus's message. But, even in his least resourceful moments, he cannot resist his tendency to exceed his brief. So he adds for good measure: 'Or come ayeyne soone after ye be wente' (IV. 934–35). Had he been able to overhear her 'heigh compleynte', he might have taken particular care to avoid even hinting at, let alone positively recommending, such a course of postponed action. On the other hand, he may half-consciously be playing the part of tempter. For when discussing with Troilus the proposed elopement, he had declared: 'if she wilneth fro the for to passe, / Thanne is she fals; so love hire wel the lasse' (IV. 615–16). That remark should certainly alert the reader to the crucial importance of the lovers' final interview.

(ii) THE CRUCIAL DEBATE

That interview begins with the episode of the 'averted tragedy', the implications of which were discussed in an earlier chapter. What concerns us now is the lovers' dispute, occupying almost the last five hundred lines of Book IV, in which Criseyde forestalls and finally rejects the proposal of abduction which was the practical purpose of Troilus's visit. The importance of this scene in the development of the plot and for its revelation of character has already been emphasised.[69] It differs from its original in *Il Filostrato* in much the same way as does the scene between Troilus and Pandarus earlier in Book IV. Boccaccio provides a debate between the lovers in which alternative courses of action are proposed and considered on their merits. Eventually Troilo accepts Criseida's plan with some reluctance. Later, in her soliloquy at the beginning of Canto VI, she admits she was mistaken in urging her plan: she now realises that in order to avoid a bad course of action she had chosen a worse. In Canto VII

Troilo, having interpreted his dream about Criseida and the boar, apostrophises her, and retrospectively finds her contribution to the debate in Canto IV full of duplicity. In Book V of *Troilus* there is nothing corresponding to this particular recrimination; but Chaucer brings forward to his representation of the debate itself a certain – or rather, an uncertain – uneasiness on the part of his hero and reports his heroine's speeches in such a way as to cause the reader to suspect her arguments of being specious and even shifty, although he supplies no palpable reasons for our doubting the genuineness of her grief at parting temporarily from her lover, nor for questioning the sincerity of her conscious intention to return on the tenth day.

The transition from the *tragédie manquée* to the debate is effected with surprising abruptness within the space of a single stanza. Eyeing Troilus's drawn sword, Criseyde resolutely declares that, if he had slain himself, she would have remained no longer alive:

> 'But with this selve swerd, which that here is,
> My selve I wolde han slayn', quod she tho;
> 'But hoo, for we han right ynough of this,
> And lat us rise and streight to bedde go,
> And there lat us speken of oure wo.
> For by the morter which that I see brenne
> Knowe I ful wel that day is not fer henne.'
> (IV. 1240–46)

The dramatic situation, and the presence of Troilus, impel her to make an unwontedly heroic gesture. Her neat turn of phrase maintains the theatrical rhetoric: 'with this *selve* swerd ... / My *selve* I wolde han slayn ...'. The cynic within us will exclaim that she can well afford to make such a gesture now that the glimpsed tragedy has been safely averted and will remind us that in her earlier *scena*, when she was alone and suicide was seriously in prospect, she had decided not to handle 'swerd ne darte ... for the crueltee'. Thus, even before the debate begins, we are prompted to wonder whether the resolutions she makes in Troilus's presence will be matched by the same firmness of purpose when she is once more on her own.

A gesture more in keeping with her true character is that with which she so abruptly dispels the now superseded drama: 'But hoo, for we han right ynough of this'. Now is not the time to contemplate the tragedy that might have been, but to forestall the one that may be. As we have seen, Criseyde, like her uncle, has a decided predilection for the practical over the romantic; but, as we are about to see, she has, unlike her uncle, little notion of what is practicable. Indeed, in pulling herself up short in this way, she is recalling his advice that, when Troilus arrives, she should endeavour to hide her sorrow and think of some plan to meet the emergency: 'Bet is a tyme of cure ay than of pleynte' (IV. 931). The influence of Pandarus is evident as soon as she begins to speak to Troilus. The first stanza of her speech is little more than an expansion of the line just quoted, and the second stanza begins with an inflation of her uncle's statement that 'Wommen ben wise in short avysement':

> 'I am a womman, as ful wel ye woot,
> And as I am avysed sodeynly,
> So wol I telle yow whil it is hoot.'
>
> (IV. 1261–63)

There are altogether six stanzas of preamble before she describes her plan inspired by her uncle's unhappy afterthought. They betray some uneasiness on her part. The *occupatio* formulas of the fourth stanza ('I wol nat make long sermoun', etc.), instead of ushering in the prologue's abridgement, lead up to a 'protestacioun' of her sincerity which draws too much attention to itself by occupying the whole of the fifth stanza. It is also undermined by her preceding request to Troilus to forgive her 'If I speke aught ayeynes youre hertes reste' (IV. 1287). When one hears from the beloved the formula 'Now I am going to say something I know will upset you', the heart sinks; for it fears that this is the prelude to the ending of the relationship. Criseyde, of course, does not consciously believe that what she is about to propose constitutes anything of the kind, but her elaborate prolegomena implant a sense of uneasiness in the reader.

Even before Troilus criticises, point by point, Criseyde's stratagem for returning to Troy, it is made evident to the reader that she has little insight into the workings of her father's mind and no appreciation of his prophetic foresight. This may be seen – to cite but one example – in the syllogism whose doubtful logic supplies the intellectual groundwork for her plan: 'My fader ... / Is olde; and elde is ful of coveytise' (IV. 1368–69); therefore, 'Desir of gold' will outweigh his faith in his oracles' 'amphibologies' – as she sceptically describes them. So, when she is exchanged for Antenor, she will take to her father the 'moeble' that she has in Troy and offer it as earnest of a 'huge quantite' to follow, if only he will permit her to return to the city and fetch it out secretly. But we have already heard Calchas declare to the Greeks that he fled from Troy, 'Havyng unto my tresour ne my rente / Right no resport' (IV. 85). He assures them that he was content 'For yow to lese al that I have in Troie ... Save of a doughter that I lefte, allas! / Slepyng at hom' (IV. 91–93).

The patent weakness of this and other parts of her strategy may lead the reader to wonder whether she may not herself be speaking in 'amphibologies'.[70] Are these arguments with which she seriously hopes to 'blende' her father? Or are they intended rather to make Troilus acquiesce in her departure without making a further 'scene'? Speaking of her father, she says:

> 'I shal hym so enchaunten with my sawes,

That right in hevene his soule is, shal he meete.'
(IV. 1395–96)

In fact it is Troilus who, after some initial misgivings, is thus 'enchaunted' into imagining himself in a dream-heaven. Admittedly, the enchantment is only in part the work of Criseyde's 'sawes'; the fact that the debate is conducted in bed allows other enchantments to make their contribution too:

> For which the grete furie of his penaunce
> Was queynt with hope; and therwith hem bitwene
> Bigan for joie thamorouse daunce.
> And as the briddes, whan the sonne is shene,
> Deliten in hire song in leves grene,
> Right so the wordes that they spake yfeere
> Delited hem, and made hire hertes clere.
> (IV. 1429–35)

But the spell binds for a single stanza only. After that the reality principle overthrows the pleasure principle in Troilus's mind and he exposes all the weaknesses in his lady's argument.

So alarmed is the awakened Troilus by her proposals that his language to her is unusually forthright and falls into a popular, proverbial idiom that we have come to associate with Pandarus: 'the bear has one intention, his trainer another'; 'don't feign lameness to a cripple, because he will see through the act'; and, more pithily, 'Men may the wise atrenne, and naught atrede' (IV. 1456). He even becomes sarcastic. In making the point that she has lamentably under-estimated her father's cunning, he alludes obliquely and contemptuously to one detail of her plan to deceive Calchas: 'he may have been deprived of his 'moeble', but he still has his 'olde sleighte' with him' (IV. 1460–61). Remembering how he has himself almost been charmed into acquiescence, he adds that her 'sex appeal' will have no effect upon her father: 'Ye shal nat blende *hym* for youre wommanhede' (IV. 1462). Indeed, if it comes to charming with words and with sex appeal, it is more likely that her father, a professional preacher ('as he kan wel preche') will 'yow glose / To ben a wyf' (IV. 1471–72) — Troilus is sarcastically reiterating the word she had used of her father at IV. 1410. Calchas will so commend the parts of 'som Grek' 'That ravysshen he shal yow with his speche', or, failing that, compel her by force.

To 'ravysshen' Criseyde — to persuade her to elope with him — is the purpose of Troilus's present speech, but he employs no 'ravishing' words — so intent is he upon his destructive criticism of her 'sleight'. He dismisses as a 'fantasye' (IV. 1470) the idea of her father's ever returning to Troy, and points out that to rely upon a plan that involves their separation on opposite sides of the military lines is tantamount to tempting Fortune. But this soldier, endowed with a philosophical turn of mind, expresses the latter notion more metaphysically: to adopt Criseyde's plan instead of his own would be equivalent to exchanging 'substaunce' for 'accident' (IV. 1505). Realising that such a philosophical distinction may be lost upon Criseyde, he translates it for her ('I mene thus:', IV. 1506) and instinctively hits upon two of the key words in Criseyde's vocabulary:

> 'Thus mene I, that it were a grete folie
> To putte that *sikernesse* in *jupartie* '.
> (IV. 1510–11)

But, as we have seen in Book II, in Criseyde's idiolect *sikernesse* is no synonym for 'elopement' or for any kind of *aventure*.[71] Indeed, for Criseyde *sikernesse* implies the quiet life, where she enjoys a respected position in society and where she can be sure that any amorous liaison that may threaten her 'name' will be kept absolutely secret. Troilus's proposal, whether it succeeds or not, is incompatible with such a definition of *sikernesse;* her own plan ensures it – whether she manages to return to Troilus or remains with her father.

Finally, Troilus makes one other act of semantic condescension for Criseyde's benefit. Though she may not appreciate the metaphysical sense of *substaunce,* her plan – with its preoccupation with *moeble* and other forms of lucre – shows that she has a solid interest in its material *sensus vulgaris.* So he assures her:

> 'And vulgarly to speken of substaunce
> Of tresour, may we bothe with us lede
> Inough to lyve in honour and plesaunce,
> Til into tyme that we shul ben dede.'
> (IV. 1513–16)

Even if they should arrive at the distant homes of his friends and kinsfolk 'in oure bare sherte', they would be well provided for and 'ben honoured while we dwelten there'. His scheme is so sound that all risks are underwritten. All that matters is: 'go we anon' (IV. 1525).

But Criseyde is even more determined that go with him she shall not. In the course of her *riposte* she shows that she is his match in the use of one particular polemical tactic; namely, that of 'picking on' salient terms from his speech and turning them against him.[72] Just as he had sarcastically thrown back at her the word *moeble,* so she tosses back his terms *fantasye* (IV. 1470) and *jupartie* (IV. 1511). After listening to his speculations about what will happen to her in the Grecian camp, and particularly as the result of the attentions of 'som Grek', she angrily accuses him of mistrusting her and exclaims: 'Drif out the *fantasies* yow withinne' (IV. 1615). In III. 1030–32 she had specifically associated 'fantasie' with 'jalousie', when admonishing him for his supposed jealousy of her on account of Horaste. At that time she was anxious to make up the quarrel, so she decided to call his passion an 'illusion', the consequence of 'habundaunce of love and besy cure' (III. 1040–42). This, unlike the repressed 'furie', is excusable — 'for the gentilesse'. Even though the quarrel is made up so that they may enter into the mutual oblivion of sexual union, she has impressed upon her mind the idea that he is susceptible to 'fantasie'; as can be seen from her use of the term at the moment of their first parting (III. 1504). Now, angered at his application of the term to her own notions, as well as by his insinuations about 'som Grek', she is confirmed in this opinion of his character and decides that no speculations that come from his brain need be seriously attended to. The penalty of Troilus's connivance, however unwillingly, at Pandarus's imposition of a deceitful fabrication upon his niece is now being exacted. The price to be paid for allowing Pandarus to deliver an incarnate goddess into his embrace is now clearly revealed. It is one of the neatest, as well as one of the bitterest, ironies in the poem.

Criseyde is particularly distressed at what she alleges to be his mistrust of her; for she had sworn to be true to him (IV. 1610). Some readers may think that she had protested too much in the course of her three stanzas (IV. 1534—54) of oaths which even invoke such small fry as those demi-gods of the desert, the Greater and Lesser Faun and Satyr. But it seems to me that there is nothing intrinsically suspect about this protestation. Certainly the appeal in her final stanza to

'... Symois, that as an arew clere
Thorugh Troie rennest ay downward to the se ...'
(IV. 1548—49)

to return to its source, should she be false, sounds poetically more convincing than would the customary calling to witness of the major deities of the classical pantheon. It is only when they are compared with Troilus's later protestation, when Criseyde in turn bids him be true to her, that these stanzas seem somewhat embroidered. For Troilus calls to witness only 'god, to whom ther nys no cause ywrye' and assures his lady that his trustworthiness 'shal be founde at preve'. It is also significant that this, his last speech in the Book (IV. 1654—59), and his preceding interjection (IV. 1597—1603), are each contained within a single stanza, whereas Criseyde is far more prolix — in contrast to her usual economy of speech in the earlier Books.

As for the second salient term that Criseyde seizes upon — 'jupartye' — she throws that back in his teeth when, at IV. 1566, she urges him to abandon his proposed flight 'or that ye *juparten* so youre name'. We considered, in an earlier chapter, the supreme importance that she attaches to her own 'name'. Her regard for its sanctity (almost as if it were her soul) is produced as the sovereign argument against Troilus's proposal at IV. 1576—82 . The fact that her approach to this sovereign stanza is by way of three that are concerned with Troilus's 'name' suggests that her solicitude for his honour is as great as her regard for her own. Her concern for his future welfare is sensible and even altruistic. The consequences that she predicts in IV. 1555—75 are indeed likely to follow upon any elopement; it will be said that Troilus has fled for cowardice and that they have eloped for 'lust voluptuous'. Moreover, she is sufficiently circumspect to recognise the possibility that a prince and a knight may ultimately regret the abdication of his social privileges, the abandonment of his military career, and the sacrifice of his 'honour', even for the sake of a true love relationship:

> 'But that ye speke, awey thus for to go
> And leten alle youre frendes, god forbede,
> *For any womman,* that ye sholden so ...'
> (IV. 1555–57)

For any woman to utter such a sentiment is in itself a little strange. But for Criseyde to speak in so detached and 'altruistic' a way about Troilus is 'straunge' in a sense almost as chilling as that in which the epithet is later applied by him to her final letter (V. 1633). What the altercation between the lovers ultimately reveals is not so much that Criseyde is 'selfish' as that for her the pearl of great price is one thing; for Troilus it is another.

Even more chilling is her conclusion: 'And forthi sle with resoun al this hete' (IV. 1583) – with which she dismisses the only plan that he believed would save their love. The cut is the unkindest of all because Troilus's ability to control passion by reason, at moments of crisis, is one of his most conspicuous virtues – and one, moreover, of which Criseyde is well aware. On several occasions he refrains from precipitate action purely out of consideration for her and for her 'name'. At the session of the Trojan 'parlement' in which the exchange of Antenor for Criseyde is debated, he is present but restrains himself from seconding Hector, who argues that there is no question of an exchange of prisoners, since Criseyde is not a prisoner, and – naming the proposed transaction by its proper name – declares: 'We usen here no wommen for to selle' (IV. 182). For the sake of his lady's 'honour' Troilus dare not speak, 'Leste men sholde his affeccioun espye'; and so *'With mannes herte* he gan his sorwe drye'. As the public debate, that leads to a thoroughly dishonourable and nationally disastrous resolution, continues around him, an interior debate between Love and Reason is fought in his mind. This interior debate leads to the honourable, but also disastrous, resolution to take no action 'Withoute assent of hire'. The same[73] consideration restrains him at IV. 540–81 when Pandarus urges him to abduct Criseyde. After stating his objections, Troilus concludes:

> 'Thus am I with desir and resoun twight;
> Desir for to destourben hire me redeth;
> And reson nyl nat, so myn herte dredeth.'
> (IV. 573–75)

Again it is Reason that prevails.[74] The moment when his interior conflict is most acute has yet to come. This is at V. 43–56 when he refrains from armed intervention as Criseyde departs from Troy escorted by Diomede.

Even as she opposes Troilus's arguments, Criseyde continues to express her affection for him. But the expression sounds a little forced and exaggerated: as can be seen if we compare IV. 1640 — 'Myn owene hertes sothfast suffisaunce' — with the line in which she originally surrendered herself to him: 'Welcome! my knyght, my pees, my suffisaunce' (III. 1309). As soon as he accedes to her plan, her acerbity of tone softens completely as she pronounces the tender panegyric of her lover, the second stanza of which concludes with the often quoted couplet:

> '... moral vertu, grounded upon trouthe,
> That was the cause I first hadde on yow routhe.'
>
> (IV. 1672–73)

More revealing of Criseyde's attitude towards Troilus's 'trouthe' is, however, the sentiment that concludes the first stanza:

> '... so trewe I have yow founde,
> That ay honour to meward shal rebounde.'
>
> (IV. 1665–66)

In other words: her 'name' will receive reflected 'honour' from his. The whole speech proves to be ambiguous in tone. The third stanza at first seems touchingly ingenuous. The slightly fumbling syntax of its opening lines — so unlike Criseyde's usually confident sentence structure — rises to the simple assurance of the concluding pomise:

> 'Ek gentil herte and manhod that ye hadde,
> And that ye hadde, as me thoughte, in despit
> Every thyng that souned into badde,
> As rudenesse and poeplissh appetit,
> *And that youre resoun bridlede youre delit,* —
> This made, aboven every creature,
> That I was youre, and shal, whil I may dure.'
>
> (IV. 1674–80)

But we have already observed what constitutes her notion of 'reasonableness'. The sense of ambivalence increases in the fourth and last stanza. The assurance given at its beginning is of monumental weight and grandeur:

> 'And this may lengthe of yeres naught fordo,
> Ne remuable Fortune deface.'
>
> (IV. 1681–82)[75]

But the vista of time shrinks, with alarming bathos, as the 'practical' Criseyde asserts herself and the argument descends through the appeal to 'Juppiter', to grant that they may be re-united before *ten nights* have passed, on to the almost brusque dismissal in the final line: 'And fare now wel, for tyme is that ye rise'. It is true that this is matched by Troilus's abrupt departure in the Book's final line:

> For whan he saugh that she ne myghte dwelle,
> Which that his soule out of his herte rente,
> Withouten more, out of the chaumbre he wente.

But there is this difference: when there is nothing more to be said, he says nothing. He will not join in her prayer to Jupiter: he has never had any faith in her ill-conceived plan. All he sees is the cruel actuality 'that she ne myghte *dwelle*'.

(iii) AFTER THE DIALOGUE

In a sense the remainder of the action follows as an anti-climax, an extended corollary of the conclusion arrived at in the debate. In Book V we experience the realisation of what is already potentially present in the ending of Book IV: the debate has diagnosed a cancer in the relationship whose lingering death we watch helplessly throughout the final Book. The sense of anti-climax in no way detracts from the poignant intensity of Troilus's story; but what we experience is the poignancy of pathos in the most literal sense of the word — passive sorrow, with a feeling of all effective action spent.

Similarly, Criseyde finds that very little scope remains to her for positive action. Her betrayal of Troilus consists of two interrelated, but distinguishable, acts: her failure to return to Troy as promised, and her yielding to Diomede. Chaucer makes it clear that she is trapped into the first of these acts and that she pays no attention to the persistent Diomede — who begins his operations much earlier than does his counterpart in *Il Filostrato* — until after her father foiled her plan to be secretly re-united with Troilus. She has been unable to unsettle his faith in what she had contemptuously called 'amphibologies': Calchas will not allow her to return to Troy, even temporarily, since he 'knows' it is doomed. The 'wys' Criseyde realises too late that it was she who had already placed herself in the snare during the debate with Troilus by rejecting his plan. Looking back ruefully upon that fatal decision, she apostrophises Prudence in a moment of almost classical *anagnorisis:*

> 'Prudence, allas, oon of thyn eyen thre
> Me lakked alwey, or that I com here.
> On tyme ypassed wel remembered me;
> And present tyme ek koude ich wel ise;
> But futur tyme, or I was in the snare,
> Koude I nat sen: that causeth now my care.'
> (V. 744—49)

But this soliloquy reveals also how imperfectly she understands herself; for the debate made it clear that her rejection of Troilus's proposal cannot be explained merely in terms of lack of prudence or foresight. Now she recognises how mistaken she was in her fears of the scandal and the damage to her 'name' that would attend upon an elopement with Troilus:

'Who myghte have seyd that I hadde don amys,
To stele awey with swich oon as he is?'
(V. 739–40)

We saw how *jupartye* was a key word in their debate: before she mentioned the potential harm to her own name she had urged Troilus to abandon his plan 'or that ye juparten so youre name'.[76] But now she must place herself in real 'jupartye', if they are to be re-united: the prospect immediately before her is not 'To stele awey with swich oon as he is', but 'To stele awey by nyght' — and by herself!

'And if that I me putte in *jupartye,*
To stele awey by nyght, and it bifalle
That I be kaught, I shal be holde a spie;
Or elles, lo, this drede I moost of alle:
If in the hondes of som *wrecche* I falle,
I nam but lost, *al be myn herte trewe* ...'
(V. 701–05)

Even this risk of innocent rape might have been worth taking rather than that of remaining in the Greek camp to fall, as she does, into the hands of a nobly born 'wrecche' who will cause her to make her 'herte [*un*] trewe'.

Criseyde's sense of the need for a champion to stand up for her in the Grecian 'coost' seems to be a piece of self-deceiving rationalisation that substitutes an imaginary need for the real one that she dare not acknowledge. She needs a love affair with 'som Grek' to protect her from Troilus — or, rather, from her lingering affection for him and from her guilt concerning her treatment of him now that she has determined to 'dwelle' with the Greeks. Her feelings for her former lover now consist of a mixture of, on the one hand, shame, remorse, regret and residual affection (V. 1072–83) and, on the other hand, an unconscious urge to desecrate their relationship so as to be psychologically released from it. So she gives Diomede the bay horse Troilus had given her and even the brooch — 'and that was litel nede' (V. 1040) — she had received from him at parting.[77] It is when Diomede is hurt through the body *by Troilus* that she offers her new lover the greatest treasure she had given the old. Having thus safely compromised herself by means of this obscene, compulsive ritual of self-immolation, she makes a pathetic attempt to exorcise the ghost of Troilus permanently from her conscience by resolving: 'To Diomede algate I wol be trewe'.

Troilus's pathetic self-deception, throughout much of this final Book, is nourished by his virtues — by his 'largesse' and 'fraunchyse', his generosity of spirit that persists in believing the best about Criseyde. This is nowhere more evident than in his reaction to Cassandra's correct interpretation of his dream about Criseyde and the boar as a revelation that 'This Diomede is inne, and thow art oute' (V. 1519). He promptly denounces his sister as a 'sorceresse' and calumniator of good women, as he demands of whoever cares to overhear him:

> 'Now sestow nat this fool of fantasie
> Peyneth hire on ladys for to lye?'
>
> (V. 1523–24)

We may properly admire his loyalty to his lady, but may wonder who is the 'fool of fantasie' when he continues:

> 'As wel thow myghtest lyen on Alceste,
> That was of creatures, but men lye,
> That evere weren, kyndest and the beste.
> For whan hire housbonde was in jupartye
> To dye hym self, but if she wolde dye,
> She ches for hym to dye and gon to helle,
> And starf anon, as us the bokes telle.'
>
> (V. 1527–33)

The ultimate effect of these lines is to point to the one thing necessary that is wanting in the love of the heroine whose beauty was originally likened to that of 'an hevenyssh perfit creature' sent down to earth. During the narrator's final act of *captatio benevolentiae,* when he apologises to the ladies for having depicted a false heroine, Alcestis is mentioned explicitly, along with Penelope, as the antithesis of Criseyde. Her supreme act of 'Agape' adumbrates the alternative to 'feyned loves' which the poet commends to the 'yonge fresshe folkes' in his Epilogue:

> And loveth hym which that right for love
> Upon a cros, oure soules for to beye,
> First starf ...
>
> (V. 1842–44)

A similar ambivalence in Chaucer's presentation of his pagan hero is to be seen in Troilus's final apostrophe to his faithless lady. When Pandarus declares that he hates his niece – and long after Diomede has urged her not to waste 'a quarter of a tere' (V. 880) on any lover in the 'prison' of Troy – Troilus declares that he cannot find it in his heart 'To unloven yow a quarter of a day' (V. 1609). His utterance may be regarded as the ultimate in erotic besottedness: the final evidence that Cupid has established a tyranny within his soul. On the other hand, there is a partial analogy between the inability of this lover to 'unloven' his erring lady and the divine Agape which is incapable of wishing uncreated any of the erring human creatures who have proved untrue to their Creator. To put it another way: if the author of *Ancrene Wisse* could have read Troilus's 'unsely aventure', he might well have exclaimed: 'Hweat þolieð men & women for fals luue & for ful luue. & mare walden þolien?'[78] Yet, in Troilus's final attitude towards Criseyde, there is a kind of analogy with one particular in which – according to the same treatise – Christ's love for the soul surpasses man's love for woman:

Muche luue is ofte bitweone mon & wummon, ah þah ha were iweddet him, ha mahte iwurðen se unwreast, & swa longe ha mahte forhorin hire wið oþre men þet, þah ha walde a ein cumen, he ne kepte hire nawt. For þi crist luueð mare: for þah þe sawle his spuse forhori hire wið þe feond under heaued sunnne feole ȝeres & dahes, his mearci is hire eauer ȝarow hwen ha wule cumen ham & leten þen deouel.[79]

But in the world where Cupid is the god of love, such sentiments are bound to end in frustration. The only hope for those who, like Troilus, 'ben despeired out of loves grace', is that they may be allowed 'soone out of this world to pace' (I. 41–42).

PART THREE
THE ENDING

Chapter Seven
The Flight from Love

When Rosalind wishes to prove to Orlando that, during the six thousand years of the world's history, no man ever died 'in his own person' for love, her first *exemplum* is Troilus, who 'had his brains dashed out with a Grecian club; yet he did what he could to die before, and he is one of the patterns of love' (*As You Like It*, IV. I. 100–3). Chaucer makes a similar point about Troilus by introducing two contexts in which the hero fails to die for love.

The first is the theatrically engineered episode of the 'averted tragedy' in Book IV, where everything is set for the lovers to achieve ultimate fulfilment in a veritable *liebestod* that would have satisfied any nineteenth-century romantic. In Chaucer's poem, however, its effect is ironical insofar as it is immediately followed by the debate which reveals so much of how little the lovers have understood of each other. When Troilus resolved upon suicide he was prepared both for death and damnation. He determines

> Hym self to sleen, how sore that hym smerte,
> So that his soule hire soule folwen myghte,
> Ther as the doom of Mynos wolde it dighte.
> $$\text{(IV. 1186–88)}$$

Chaucer would have known Minos, not only as the infernal judge of classical mythology, but as 'conoscitor delle peccata' of *Inferno* V. 9, who assigns the already damned souls to the appropriate circle for their punishment. The prisoners of the Second Circle (who share with Minos the same Canto V) are the 'carnal sinners who subject reason to desire' ('i peccator carnali / che la ragion sommettono al talento' [V. 38–39]). Their company contains several of the famous lovers of legend and of history – including Dido, Cleopatra, Pyramus and Thisbe – who had committed suicide for love. Minos is associated with the punishment of suicides in particular at *Inferno* XIII. 96 – a canto already mentioned on account of its presentation of Piero delle Vigne.[80] Suicide for love may be accounted the extreme instance of subordinating reason to desire. As early as I. 823–24 Troilus himself had recognised it as a 'synne'. We have seen[81] how, on several occasions in Book IV, Troilus controls passion with 'Resoun'. It is interesting to find that, on the one occasion in that Book when he is determined to take the extreme opposite course, he is prevented from doing anything so desperate.

The second occasion when Troilus fails to die for love occurs at the story's end, when he determines to be revenged upon Diomede (V. 1702—3) and to seek his own death in arms (V. 1718). But, though the rivals inflict many wounds upon each other,

> ... Fortune it naught ne wolde
> Of otheres hond that eyther deyen sholde.
>
> (V. 1763—64)

So the 'tragedye' ends with the receding spectacle of the now indistinguishable silhouettes of Troilus and Diomede locked in futile and inconclusive combat — just as Criseyde is locked in the Greek's embrace. Many twentieth-century readers may find this 'existentialist' hell, with the rivals left repeatedly 'clapper-clawing' each other — as Shakespeare's Thersites would say — even more gruesomely apt than that of the tempest-tossed souls of *Inferno* V.

These same readers may wish that Chaucer had ended the poem at this point. But, for the second time, Troilus is prevented from dying for love: this time by nothing other than his death. For he dies, not as part of the personal vendetta into which the 'tragedye' of his 'lovynge of Criseyde' has degenerated, but — like Hector — at the hands of his country's most formidable enemy. The announcement of his death (V. 1800—6) is separated from the account of his skirmishes with Diomede by five stanzas in which the poet begins the process of 'turning up the house lights' by addressing the male and then the female members of the audience and by apostrophising 'litel myn tragedye'. His first gesture of *captatio benevolentiae,* addressed presumably to the men, apologises for the fact that he has said hardly anything about 'The armes of this ilke worthi man' (V. 1765). So the manner in which Troilus's death is introduced seems to extricate it from the 'litel ... tragedye' of his 'unsely aventure' and to place it in the context of a glorious epic about the Trojan hero second only to Hector — but an epic which the poet has chosen not to write.

It is a curious fact that, on both occasions when Troilus is prevented from dying 'in a love-cause', the result is attributed (parenthetically) to divine intervention. At IV. 1212 Criseyde revives from her swoon 'as god wolde'; at V. 1805—6 the communiqué announcing Troilus's death states:

> But, weilawey, *save only goddes wille!*
> Ful pitously hym slough the fierse Achille.[82]

How much weight these parenthetical ejaculations carry is uncertain: there are several instances of similar phrases in the poem that are little more than empty asseverations. All that we are entitled to remark is that, at the end of Chaucer's narrative, Troilus's soul — unlike those of the lovers 'che la ragion sommettono al talento' — is allotted its eternal abode, not by Minos, but by Mercury (V. 1826—27), the Psychopomp of classical mythology or — in E. M. Forster's memorable phrase — the 'conductor of souls to a not too terrible hereafter'.

Because the three stanzas that describe Troilus's visit to the Ogdoad and Mercury's disposal of his soul are not contained in all manuscripts, scholars have argued that they may be part of a revision of the poem. However that may be, it cannot be denied that they constitute an integral part of the poem's partly symmetrical scheme: the hero's celestial laughter (V. 1821) corresponds to, and is contrasted with, his scornful smiling at lovers when he is first introduced into the narrative (I. 194). By what precise eschatalogical process, and with what positive theological justification, he arrives at this celestial vantage point has been the subject of much learned conjecture.[83] But Chaucer has nothing to say on this question; all he is concerned with is Troilus's attitude as he looks down upon 'This litel spot of erthe, that with the se / Embraced is' (V. 1815–16). Perhaps it is imperceptive of me to feel that there is something complacently negative and blandly simplistic about Troilus's attitude of *contemptus mundi* as he looks down from the eighth sphere: but it must be admitted that the disembodied 'goost' is a lesser figure than the hero of the 'tragedye'. As he ascends, he may seem to jettison much that was bound up in the subtle knot that made him man whereas, throughout the drama, Chaucer had presented his character, no less than Criseyde's, as a knot too 'intrinse t'unloose'.

It may seem that in the end Troilus has not advanced but retreated: his heavenward flight is a flight from experience and a reversion to the condition in which he is discovered when he is first introduced into the action before Cupid strikes and he steps on to Fortune's escalator. It is true that the pointed correspondence between these two episodes implies an advance in one respect. The scornful smiling and open taunts in Book I betray the amused arrogance of the man who is ignorant of what he despises, whereas his celestial laughter 'in hym self' (V. 1821) represents the benevolent amusement of a soul at those who consider his death a cause for weeping. But what really matters is that he is confirmed in his pristine position, with the difference that he is now immune from the traumatic contacts with Cupid and Fortune. No doubt a 'psycho-analytical' critic will see in his entering 'the holughnesse of the eighte spere' (V. 1809) a symbol of his return to the safety of the womb. Though we may dismiss the symbolic interpretation as merely fortuitous and capricious, the point that it makes is not without validity.

In order to make a more positive impression, it would have been necessary for the eschatalogical episode to present an advance from 'carnal' and erotic love to divine love. Since Troilus was always inclined to take a transcendental view of love, to feel himself bound to his lady by the principle of love that binds the whole of creation in harmony, such an advance would have seemed appropriate. But in the course of these three stanzas (V. 1807–27) there is no mention of love: the heaven which Troilus enters is impersonal, scientific and philosophical. He sees 'with ful avysement, / The erratik sterres' and hears the music of the spheres; he glimpses the 'pleyn felicite / That is in hevene above' (in other words what Boethius calls the 'summum bonum' − a generalised, philosophical notion). What is more, we are given the impression that the eighth sphere is uninhabited − unlike those of Dante's paradise, which are filled with souls or angelic beings who reflect the divine love. Although Troilus perceives the harmony of the spheres, he does not feel his desire and his will revolved by 'l'amor che move il sole e l'altre stelle'.

Here we can no longer ignore the fact that Chaucer is up against a theological difficulty in presenting the ultimate fate of his pagan hero. Sufficient literary precedents could be cited for propelling a pagan's soul, with reasonable assurance and in tolerable comfort, to one of the heavenly spheres; but for him to experience the personal love of the Christian God is another matter. The nearest personality in time and place from among these precedents is that other Trojan, Ripheus − in fact 'the Troian daun Ripheo' whom Chaucer happens to mention in passing at IV. 53. This Virgilian character finds his way into the twentieth canto of the *Paradiso* because 'tutto suo amor là giù pose a drittura' (121) − while he was on earth he set all his love on righteousness so that Divine Grace opened his eyes to the Christian revelation, even though he was a pagan living a thousand years before the Incarnation. But Dante is at pains to maintain that both he and his companion in beatitude, Trajan, did not issue from their bodies as pagans ('gentili'); they were already Christians while in the flesh (XX. 103−4). This is their essential difference from Troilus. Although the story of his 'lovynge of Criseyde' reveals something of his 'potential' for transcendental love, it could never be focused upon the Person that a Christian would regard as the only proper object of such love. Chaucer must defer his invocation of the love of Christ as the alternative to 'feyned loves' until he addresses his Christian audience of potential lovers in the Epilogue.

Chapter Eight
From Prologue to Epilogue

After he has watched Mercury conduct the hero's soul to an undisclosed (but presumably not unhappy) abode, the poet returns to earth to witness the passing of his funeral *cortège*. The tolling of his knell is heard in the anaphoric lines that pass in review his various worldly dignities and aspirations, which now appear as the particulars of 'the blynde lust, the which that may nat laste' (V. 1824):

> Swich fyn hath, lo, this Troilus for love!
> Swich fyn hath al his grete worthynesse!
> Swich fyn hath his estat real above!
> Swich fyn his lust! swich fyn hath his noblesse!
> (V. 1828–31)

These lines, including the *anaphora,* are translated from Boccaccio. In the next line *anaphora* is the only thing the two poets have in common. Chaucer writes: 'Swich fyn hath false worldes brotelnesse!'; Boccaccio has:

> Cotal fin' ebbe la speranza vana
> Di Troilo in Criseida villana.

— in other words: 'Swich fyn hath false wommenes brotelnesse!'; but Chaucer is beyond apportioning blame to his creatures.

After this solemn formality the stanza concludes with a marvellous *diminuendo* into two lines that retain the summary manner of Boccaccio's, but are altogether purged of his indignant moral posturing:

> And thus bigan his lovyng of Criseyde,
> As I have told, and in this wise he deyde.

One reason why this couplet conveys such a sense of completeness, and of all passion spent, is that it affords yet another echo of the beginning of the poem, harking back even further than did the echo from the eighth sphere. It is a transformation of that concluding couplet of the Prohemium to Book I, where the poet at last brings himself to mention his heroine and speaks of 'the double sorwes'

> Of Troilus in lovynge of Criseyde,
> And how that she forsook hym or she deyde.
> (I. 55–56)

At the outermost extremities of the poem's structure stands, like a veritable Primum Mobile, the contrast between the whole Prohemium to

Book I (which also acts as Prologue to the entire poem) and the final exhortation to 'yonge fresshe folkes, he or she' which constitutes the poem's Epilogue. The Epilogue's function cannot be adequately appreciated unless it is considered in relation to that Prologue.

The Prologue, no less than the Epilogue, is devoutly religious: whereas the Epilogue declares allegiance to the religion of Christ and Mary, the Prologue is spoken by one who has always subscribed to that of Cupid and Venus. Adapting the Papal title of 'servus servorum dei', this speaker describes himself as '... I, that god of loves servauntes serve' (I. 15) through his pious labour in writing this story of love; and at I. 29 the Prologue assumes the form of a 'bidding prayer', urging its audience to pray for various categories of lovers. A notable difference between Prologue and Epilogue is that, whereas the stanzas that follow the narration of the 'litel tragedye' are confident and hopeful, those that advertise it in advance are gloomy and despondent. Not only does the poet invoke, as his muse, the Fury 'Thesiphone', but he also declares that he dare not pray to Love to grant him any success because: 'So fer am I from his help in derknesse' (I. 18). Nor that his disqualification is a very great disadvantage in view of the sufferings of those who are able to serve the god direct. This prelude to the poem is composed almost entirely in the minor mode. On the two occasions when it modulates into a major key it stays there only briefly. At I. 22 the poet addresses '... ye loveres, that bathen in gladnesse'; but by the stanza's end he declares that, if they have never experienced suffering, then they are not genuine lovers. At I. 43 he requests his audience: '... biddeth ek for hem that ben at ese'; but again, by the stanza's end the poet has returned to the position where he conceives of his service for lovers as to 'write hire wo'.

During the narrative proper the poet continues to write from the point of view of a humanist student of antiquity who is also a non-participating devotee of Cupid and his craft.[84] In spite of the frequent anachronisms — which, for the most part, merely follow the familiar medieval practice of substituting the modern analogue for the antique institution — the picture of the pagan civilisation of Troy is remarkably consistent. Although Chaucer gives us the pagan antiquity of a poet's imagination rather than that of the archaeologist's spade, his possession of a sense of history is evident from the Prologue to Book II, where he observes that fashions in love-making change from one age to another just as linguistic usages do (II. 22–35). But Chaucer is less concerned with such differences in usage than with the fact that in former times men 'spedde as wel in love as men now do' (II. 26). The equation is reversible: it implies that the 'loveres' to whom the poem is addressed might just as well be living in ancient Troy as in fourteenth-century London (sometimes called 'New Troy').[85] Their personal religion is substantially the same as that of the principal actors in the 'tragedye': the differences between the official, institutional religious practices of the respective civilisations are — until the Epilogue — seen as almost irrelevant 'accidents'. The anachronisms help to minimise these differences.

As the action becomes more cheerful, the devotee of Cupid conveniently suspends his knowledge of love's miseries that he had bewailed in the Prologue to Book I. He now celebrates the joy and the omnipotence of love and its deity — most enthusiastically in the Prologue to Book III and most extravagantly in the notorious blasphemies at III. 1317–23 and 1688–94. Yet, even at these supreme moments of erotic bliss, the religious cult of Cupid and Venus is subtly undermined.

The hymn to Venus, that constitutes the Prologue to Book III, is based upon lines which, in *Il Filostrato,* are attributed to Troilo. The universality of the goddess's power is celebrated in the lines:

> In hevene and helle, in erthe and salte see,
> Is felt thi myght, if that I wel descerne;
> As man, brid, best, fisshe, herbe and grene tree
> The fele in tymes with vapoure eterne.

(III. 8–11)

One is reminded of the similar universality of the harmonising power of Nature in *The Parlement of Foules:*

> Nature, the vicaire of the almyghty Lord,
> That hot, cold, hevy, lyght, moyst and dreye
> Hath knyt by evene noumbres of accord.

(379–81)

Like Venus, Nature incites all living things to sexual union, though for the specific purpose of 'engendrure'. But, whereas Nature acts as God's deputy in the physical realm, Venus's power — according to her votary — knows no bounds: 'God loveth, and to love wol nat werne', he continues. So Venus is apparently identified with Love in its absolute and supreme sense, comprehending not only the Christian notion that 'God is love' (I. John, iv. 8; 16), but also the bolder notion expressed, for example, in *Ancrene Wisse:*

> Swa ouer swiðe he luueð luue, þet he makeð hire his euening.
> ʒet ich dear segge mare: he makeð hire his meistre, &
> deð al þet ha hat as þah he moste nede.[86]

Is this to be understood merely as a piece of hyperbole on the part of Venus's committed encomiast? Or are we truly in the presence of the Venus who was to be hymned by the renaissance Platonists and depicted by Botticelli? Is this prologue's Venus compounded of Venus Urania and Venus Pandemos?[87] Are Eros and Agape ultimately identical?[88]

If such questions tease us as we read this stanza, we will look in vain for any obvious or unequivocal answer from Chaucer. Neither here nor anywhere else in his works does he ascend the Platonic ladder of love or trace the process whereby a young man's idealised, romantic passion for a

Beatrice is sublimated into a thirst for the revelation of divine love. We have noted how Criseyde is endowed with a supernatural-seeming beauty that is capable of inspiring her beholder with thoughts of paradise and of causing Troilus to feel 'a newe qualitee' in life; but the responsibilities of such beauty prove to be too great for the human heroine to bear. Whereas the ending of Criseyde's story is pathetic and unsettles our faith in earthly love, so the next of the stanzas in praise of the goddess is somewhat bathetic, and brings out implicitly the differences between the operations of an autonomous Venus and those of the Christian God. The way in which 'Joves doughter deere' exhibits her power over the highest deity comes close to the manner of domestic farce:

> Ye Joves first to thilke effectes glade,
> Thorough which that thynges lyven alle and be,
> Comeveden, and amoreux [hym] made
> On mortal thyng, and as yow list, ay ye
> Yeve hym in love ese or adversitee;
> And in a thousand formes down hym sente
> For love in erthe, and whom yow list, he hente.
>
> (III. 15—21)

In causing her father to act almost like a vulgar incubus, her behaviour is as mischievous as that of an Oberon. Readers of Ovid would have recalled that the 'thousand formes' into which the amorous Jove metamorphosed himself included those of a bull, a swan and a golden shower. But fourteenth-century readers with a taste for mythology would also be familiar with the allegorisations of pagan myths to be found in such works as the *Ovide Moralisé* or Boccaccio's own *Genealogia Deorum Gentilium.*[89] They would not have been slow to appreciate the analogy and the contrast between Jove's antics here described and the way in which Love caused the Christian God to metamorphose Himself into a helpless mortal in order to sacrifice Himself for love of mankind. The descent to earth of this Love is hymned by Lady Holychurch in a celebrated passage in *Piers Plowman*, B. i. 151—56:

> For heuene myʒt nouʒte holden it · it was so heuy of hym-self,
> Tyl it hadde of the erthe · yeten his fylle,
> And whan it haued of this folde · flesshe and blode taken,
> Was neuer leef vpon lynde · liʒter ther-after,
> And portatyf and persant · as the poynt of a nedle,
> That myʒte non armure it lette · ne none heiʒ walles.

The pattern of subversion in this Prologue is so subtle that many readers may wonder whether it is there at all. Somewhat more obvious, but still merely implicit, is the criticism of the 'heaven' of erotic love that is conveyed in the narrator's extravagant interjections at the very moment when hero and heroine consummate their love (III. 1317—23; 1688—94). Blasphemous utterances of this kind are common enough in medieval love poetry,[90] but they are here exploited satirically — at the narrator's expense. Such hyperbolical accounts of the 'felicite' of sexual union could be ejaculated only by somebody who had never experienced it: 'This passeth every wit for to devyse' (III. 1689). The narrator appears comically inept in his curiously androgynous attitude:

> O blysful nyght, of hem so longe isought,
> How blithe *unto hem bothe two* thow were!
> Why ne hadde I swich oon with my soule ybought,
> Ye, or the leeste joie that was there?

(III. 1317—20)

His use of (celestial) 'felicite' as an 'inexpressibility *topos*' (III. 1691—92) at the moment of the lovers' greatest ecstasy also proves to be an embarrassment to the reader. By the time the narrator bids farewell to his 'litel ... tragedye' he has himself become embarrassed (V. 1765—99) as he apologises to his audience of romance-readers for having entertained them with something that he fears may have outraged their ideals. Within a few stanzas he finds himself in the pulpit addressing them as Christians.

It seems to be a reasonable assumption that the paternal tone of the concluding exhortation to 'yonge fresshe folkes' represents the authentic voice of the poem's middle-aged author. When, in the Prologue, he addressed the same audience as his contemporaries, he spoke of Love's servants merely '*As though* I were hire owne brother dere' (I. 51); and, although writing as a disabled votary of love, he had no illusions about the misery to which a man's service of that god can bring him. The Christian ending may therefore seem to be pre-ordained. Yet, in placing the narrative between a Prologue and an Epilogue that declare allegiance to opposed religions, Chaucer deploys one dogma to keep another at bay so that no explicitly Christian criticism of the narrative is allowed to affect its telling. The dogma of Cupid's religion, first acknowledged in the Prologue, is finally eroded by the narrative on its own terms. Cupid's 'proces' reveals him ultimately as a vindictive tyrant: he never had a more faithful servant than the converted Troilus; and he never rewarded anyone more cruelly. The doctrinal vacuum thus created is eventually filled by the Christian *moralitas*.

The Epilogue is, then, in competition with the dogma of the Prologue, not with the narrative that is suspended between the two dogmatic affirmations. To conclude this study, I shall consider how the poetry of the Epilogue enacts its own ritual drama, in which the sense of Christ's love becomes increasingly intense until the presence of Jesus and his mother is felt so intimately that it becomes far more 'real' than that of the god of Love (or his mother) whose power the speaker of the Prologue recognises.

When Christian love is eventually commended as the only true and lasting love, two aspects of the loving God are presented in successive stanzas: in the first stanza of the Epilogue He is seen as Creator; in the second as Redeemer. The rejected alternative to true love is, however, described in much less specific terms. In the second stanza it is simply designated 'feyned loves' (V. 1848), and in the first it is not even specified as love at all: what the young people are urged to eschew is 'worldly vanyte' (V. 1837) – just as Troilus, when looking down from his celestial station, does not 'despise' wordly love specifically, but simply regards all earthly aspirations as 'vanite [emptiness] / To respect of the pleyn [full] felicite' that he now glimpses (V. 1816–19).

This memorable first stanza of the Epilogue achieves its appeal by combining a surface simplicity with a complex pattern of sounds and a subtle allusiveness of meaning. Chaucer's adaptation of Boccaccio in this stanza requires little comment: he includes both sexes in his address; he removes all sense of recrimination; he simplifies 'amoroso disio' to 'love'; he adds the epithet 'fresshe', which alliterates with 'folkes', and he allows its second syllable a lengthened echo in the rhyme-word 'she'. Although the beauty of these 'yonge fresshe folkes, he or she' will pass away, like the world itself and the 'floures faire' of the stanza's cadence, there is no suggestion here of woman's love turned sour or that 'lilies that fester smell far worse than weeds'.

More significant than the poet's modifications of his principal source, however, is the contrast between his mode of addressing his audience here and the way in which he addressed them in the Prologue. The lines:

> O yonge fresshe folkes, he or she,
> In which that love up groweth with your age –

are not just an ornamental periphrasis for 'ye loveres' of I. 22. Although the Epilogue's exhortation to young people may sound paternal, it is the Prologue's mode of address that is the more patronising; for there is something condescending in referring to people as 'lovers' – or 'workers', 'students' or 'consumers'. There is more dignity and respect for the total human personality in the address to 'yonge fresshe folkes, he or she'. The next line places sexual love in its proper perspective: it is seen as part of a natural process: its onset and increase – the way it 'up groweth' – is accepted as part of our ordinary, healthy process of 'growing up'. The epithet 'fresshe' not only adds a note of innocence altogether absent in Boccaccio's lines, but affords a salutary contrast with the hedonistic indulgence (like a sojourn in Venusberg) that is perhaps implied in the Prologue's address to 'ye loveres, that bathen in gladnesse' (I. 22).

In the Prologue sexual love is seen as a religious cult; successful earthly love is the *summum bonum.* In the narrative the cult of an autonomous Cupid and Venus is seen to lead to an ambivalent destination, as in the central episode of *The Parlement of Foules.* There it leads both to the well of grace and the 'were' (fish-trap), to an earthly paradise and the sinister temple of Venus where the stories are depicted of those whom tyrannical love has undone – including Troilus.[91] So the episode concludes with the couplet:

Alle these were peynted on that other syde,
And al here love, and in what plyt they dyde.
(293–94)

– the cadence is similar to that which concludes the narrative of *Troilus* at
V. 1833–34. In the final episode of the *Parlement*, the courtship of the
birds on St. Valentine's day is placed under the 'yerde', or government, of
the goddess Nature, who is described – as in the portrait of Virginia
discussed earlier[92] – as 'vicaire of the almyghty lord'. To her is delegated
the creation of the physical part of the universe: she presides over both the
creation of the species and over the processes of procreation that
perpetuate them. Sexual love – including the *fine amour* pursued by the
courtly eagles – is in this way associated with the purpose of the
Creator.[93] It is in a similar perspective that human love is viewed at the
beginning of the Epilogue to *Troilus*. But Chaucer goes further. Although
he erects no Platonic ladder of love in this stanza, he implies, by means of
subtle verbal patterning, that the proper progress of human love consists of
an advance from love for the created to love for the Creator:

O yonge fresshe folkes, he or she,
In which that love *up groweth* with youre age,
Repeyreth hom fro worldly vanyte,
And of youre herte *up casteth* the visage
To thilke god that after his ymage
Yow made.

An interest in the intruded 'worldly vanyte' (of the third line) – including
the idolatrous cult of Cupid and Venus – is thus seen as a branching away
from the true process of growth. The contrast with the restrictive mode of
addressing the audience in the Prologue is now complete: Chaucer
addresses himself to the total human personality in referring to what
bestows upon it its supreme dignity, as it was understood by a
fourteenth-century Christian.

In these lines the Creator is seen not only as the proper object of
mature love, but also of nostalgia. When Troilus enters the heavenly
region, he does so merely as a tourist who is allowed a brief period to
survey the starry region round, as from the top of Fiesole with optic glass,
before the Eternal Courier hurries him away to his lodging in some
unnamed *viale* or *vicolo*. The 'yonge fresshe folkes', on the other hand,
have inherited the heavenly country – however unfairly – as their
birthright through baptism: it was a commonplace of patristic and
medieval writings to refer to our life on earth as an exile from Heaven, our
true *patria*. Troilus ultimately perceives the insignificance of the only
homeland he had ever known – 'This litel spot of erthe, that with the se /
Embraced is' (V. 1815–16) – and despises all its aspirations as vanity.
When the young people of the Epilogue are urged to abandon worldly
vanity, it is with a more powerful and positive nostalgia that exerts its pull

in the opposite direction: 'Repeyreth *hom* fro worldly vanyte' (V. 1837). Chaucer can hardly have been unaware of the fact that *repeyren* is derived ultimately from *re-patriare*. Analysed logically, therefore, 'Repeyreth hom' is tautologistic; but, experienced as poetry, the magnetic pull of the monosyllabic noun of native origin through the trisyllabic verb of romance origin is irresistible. In V. 1839—40 the sense of returning to our fatherland is reinforced by the implied notion of the return to our Father who made us in his image. Here again the organisation of the verse enacts the sense:

> And of youre herte up casteth the visage
> To thilke god that after *his* ymage
> *Yow made* ...

We may, however, feel that the visual image in V. 1838—39 is less felicitous: we may even suspect that the curious locution 'And of youre herte up casteth the visage' is merely dictated by the need to find a rhyme for *age* and *ymage*. A moment's reflection will show that this is not so: Chaucer regularly uses 'corage' as a synonym for 'herte' and so could easily have written:

> And stedfastliche up casteth youre corage
> To thilke god that after his ymage ...

Nor is the phrase a piece of quirkishness peculiar to Chaucer. If the reader thinks the expression 'the heart's face' is in bad taste, what will he make of the following?—

> Circumcise therefore the foreskin of your heart, and be no
> more stiffnecked.

That is Holywrit (Deuteronomy, x. 16).[94] Part of our distaste for 'Lift up your heart's face' may be due to our familiarity with the simpler expression in liturgical use: 'Lift up your hearts' — '*sursum corda*'. But if one pauses to visualise — in one's mind's eye — this metaphorical action it may seem even more incongruous than that implied in Chaucer's phrase. Looked at more positively, the metaphor here implies the action of focusing our love upon God instead of allowing our gaze and our desires to droop downwards to the earth like those of four-footed beasts. Moreover, the rhyming of '[youre] ... visage' with 'his ymage', at the first point in the stanza where rhymes occur in adjacent lines, reinforces the idea of 'looking your heavenly Father in the face'. So the phrasing makes its contribution to the stanza's dominant note of nostalgia: its notion of the return of potentially prodigal sons and daughters from Vanity Fair to their true fatherland and the love of their heavenly Father.

When, in the Epilogue's second stanza, God is seen as Redeemer rather than Creator, Chaucer confines direct reference to love to the outer lines: to the exhortation in the first line to return Christ's love and the beautifully articulated rhetorical question, with its emphasis upon His meekness, that forms the concluding couplet. The modern reader may find the language of the inner lines unattractively mercenary and legalistic. The phrase 'oure soules for to beye' merely shows how business-like the medieval doctrine of the Atonement was; but it is the following couplet that the reader may find disconcerting:

> For he nyl falsen no wight, dar I seye,
> That wol his herte al holly on hym leye.
>
> (V. 1845—46)

It may be objected against this couplet that the condition imposed in its second line detracts from the generosity expressed in its first: the Almighty is seen as calculating, like some pettier King Lear, the quantity of proffered love before He will commit Himself to His part of the bargain.

I suspect that such an objection will be, however, largely the result of reading the lines with the wrong emphasis:

> For he nyl falsen *no wight,* dar I seye,
> That wol his herte *al holly* on hym leye.

The context shows that the proper way of reading the line is rather:

> For *he* nyl falsen no wight, dar I seye,
> That wol his herte al holly on *hym* leye.

In other words: Christ betrays nobody; only if one sets one's heart upon 'feyned loves' will one be 'falsed'. Since the poet obviously has Troilus in mind, it may be taken for granted that he is thinking only of absolutely sincere and undivided love, whether in the service of an autonomous and tyrannical Cupid ('feyned loves') or of Christ. It is this absolute quality of Troilus's love that renders it worthy to be compared, even adversely, with the love that Christ demands from the Christian soul. The thing that is most abhorrent to Christ, as well as to the author of a romance of *fine amour,* is lukewarm love. We may recall how *Ancrene Wisse* observes, citing Revelation iii. 15—16:

> Ich walde, he seið to his leofmon, þet tu were i mi luue, oðer
> allunge cald, oðer hat mid alle: ah for þi þet tu art ase wlech
> bitweone twa, nowðer hat ne cald, þu makest me to wleatien,
> & ich wulle speowe þe ut. bute þu wurðe hattre.[95]

We might expect that, after this exhortation to love Christ, Chaucer would modulate straight into the customary concluding prayer towards which the Epilogue is moving. But two acts of preparation — one public, the other personal — are interposed while the poet is on the very threshold of prayer. The narrative has allowed much scope for the activities of pagan deities; but now it is time for them to be banished from the sacred ground. The dynamic marking at the beginning of the next stanza is *forte* and the persistent *anaphora* of its denunciatory clauses echoes the rhythm of a *sanctus* bell, rung to scatter the evil spirits from the spot where the act of worship is to take place:

> Lo here, of payens cursed olde rites!
> Lo here, what alle hire goddes may availle!
> Lo here, thise wrecched worldes appetites!
> Lo here, the fyn and guerdoun for travaille
> Of Jove, Appollo, of Mars, of swich rascaille!

The same *anaphora* introduces the final couplet; but, as in the final couplet of that earlier stanza which is dominated by the same tolling figure (V. 1828—34), there is a moving *diminuendo* in the cadence:

> Lo here, the forme of olde clerkes speche
> In poetrie, if ye hire bokes seche!

Chaucer feels a kinship with these 'olde clerkes'; mention of their books causes him to think, in the first line of the next stanza, of the fate of his own. When the Christian felt the end of his life approaching, he made his will, appointing executors for the disposal of his worldly goods and committing his soul to Christ. So the poet, at the end of this long work, appoints his literary executors, 'moral Gower' and 'philosophical Strode', and then, observing his own exhortation to his audience two stanzas earlier, he adds:

> And to that *sothfast Crist, that starf on rode,*
> With *al myn herte* of mercy evere I preye
> And to the Lord right thus I speke and seye:
> (V. 1860—62)

Alternation between the formal and the intimate, between *forte* and *piano* utterances, is a telling feature of this Epilogue; and it occurs again in the concluding prayer itself. This opens with a solemn invocation of the Trinity: a formal prayer, magnificently clothed in harmonious phrases borrowed from Dante. The more subtle figures of antithesis and chiasmus now replace the simple hammer-blows of *anaphora* that characterised the earlier formal utterances:

> Thow oon, and two, and thre, eterne on lyve,
> That regnest ay in thre, and two, and oon,
> Uncircumscript, and al maist circumscrive,
> Us from visible and invisible foon
> Defende ...

Addresses to the Trinity are bound to be somewhat awesome and formal. But now, for the last time, Chaucer's tone becomes intimate — as happened on each of the earlier occasions when he referred to Christ. On the first of these occasions He is not named — a periphrasis involving a pronoun and a subordinate clause is employed: 'loveth hym which that right for love ...'. On the second occasion (V. 1860) He is named, but by His more formal title, and is kept at a distance by the use of a demonstrative: 'And to that sothfast Crist, that starf on rode' — the subordinate clause from the earlier periphrasis survives, but in a greatly simplified form. In the poem's final couplet Chaucer addresses Him direct by His most intimate name and sees Him, not as a Person of the Trinity, but as the son of an earthly mother:

> So make us, Jesus, for thi mercy digne,
> For love of mayde and moder thyn benigne.

107

1. All quotations from *Tr & C* are from R. K. Root (ed.), *The Book of Troilus and Criseyde* (Princeton, 1926). All quotations from Chaucer's other works are from F. N. Robinson (ed.), *The Works of Geoffrey Chaucer* (2nd ed., London, 1957). All italics in quotations from Chaucer are mine. On the poem's title, see Root, p. xi.

2. I consider the poem's relationship to its sources only where this is immediately relevant to my argument. For a systematic study of Chaucer's adaptation of *Il Filostrato*, see S. B. Meech, *Design in Chaucer's Troilus* (Syracuse, New York, 1959). See also C. S. Lewis, *E & S*, XVII (1932), 56–75; Dorothy Everett, *Essays on Middle English Literature* (Oxford, 1955), pp. 115 ff.; C. Muscatine, *Chaucer and the French Tradition* (Berkeley and Los Angeles, 1957), pp. 124 ff; Elizabeth Salter in J. Lawlor (ed.), *Patterns of Love and Courtesy* (London, 1966), pp. 86–106 – who argues that 'Chaucer ... is only too willing to work for local effectiveness at the expense of total consistency and continuity' (p. 90). The standard edition of *Il Filostrato* will be found in V. Branca (ed.), *Tutte le Opere di Giovanni Boccaccio,* Vol. 2 (Milan, 1964). The most convenient text for the English reader to consult is: *The Filostrato of Giovanni Boccaccio: A Trans. with Parallel Text by N. E. Griffin and A. B. Myrick* (Philadelphia, 1929). For an English translation alone, see R. K. Gordon, *The Story of Troilus* (New York, 1964) – which also contains translated excerpts from Benoit de Sainte Maure. For Chaucer's possible use of a French intermediary, see R. A. Pratt, *SP*, LIII (1956), 609–39. On other sources, see editions by Root and Robinson.

3. C. Muscatine, *Chaucer and the French Tradition* (Berkeley and Los Angeles, 1957), p. 164: my italics. For comment on a more elaborate and extreme symbolic interpretation of character and action, see below, Note 43.

4. (*Inf.* XIII. 76–78): '... and if either of you return to the world let him establish my memory, which still lies under the blow that envy gave it' (trans. J. D. Sinclair – London, 1939).

5. The further irony in Dante that Frederick (Stupor Mundi) is also consigned to Hell (*Inf.* X. 119) does not affect my argument.

6. Cf. Edmond Faral, *Les Arts Poétiques du XIIᵉ et du XIIIᵉ Siècles* (Paris, 1924), pp. 75 ff. For an English translation of Geoffrey of Vinsauf's *Nova Poetria*, see J. J. Murphy (ed.), *Three Medieval Rhetorical Arts* (Berkeley, Los Angeles, London, 1971), especially pp. 53 ff. But Vinsauf's treatment of the description of female beauty is perfunctory.

7. Several of the portraits of Criseyde discussed below have been considered by other critics; most notably by E. T. Donaldson, *Speaking of Chaucer* (London, 1970), pp. 53–59, who is particularly interested in the attitudes of the narrator towards her (on which see further, Note 8).

8. Cf. P. Dronke, *Medieval Latin and the Rise of European Love-Lyric* (Oxford, 1965), vol. I, *passim,* but especially references in his Index (vol. II, p. 600) under 'divine', 'divinity'.

9. Text from E. V. Gordon (ed.), *Pearl* (Oxford, 1953), 747–54.

10. See I. Bishop, *Pearl in its Setting: A Critical Study of the Structure and Meaning of the Middle English Poem* (Oxford, 1968) for the interpretation here adopted and for the subsequent comparisons with the function of Dante's Beatrice.

11. Cf. *Pearl,* 435; Carleton Brown (ed.), *Religious Lyrics of the XVth Century* (Oxford, 1939), No. 81, line 1 (p. 119). Both uses are applied to the Virgin.

12. This is a subtle improvement upon Boccaccio's account of her stance. Cf. the

phrase 'ay under shames drede' (I. 180) in the first part of the description.

13. See above, p. 12.

14. A 'psycho-analytical' critic will be disappointed to find that the poem never asks what he would regard as the most important question about this unhappy son of Priam: What's he to 'Ecuba'; what's 'Ecuba' to him?

15. On the aesthetic estimation of joined eyebrows in the fourteenth century, see Root (ed.), p. 544; and T. B. Hanson, *N & Q,* CCXVI (1971), pp. 285–86, who also considers the possible physiognomical significance of this feature.

16. Cf. J. Speirs, *Chaucer the Maker* (London, 1951), p. 79 – and repeated by several commentators.

17. For English trans. of Andreas's *De Amore,* see J. J. Parry, *The Art of Courtly Love* (New York, 1941). See p. 134 for the relevant commandment of the God of Love.

18. *Ibid.,* p. 31. For a notable Chaucerian use of the fishing metaphor outside the present poem, see *Complaint of Mars,* 236 ff.

19. For a rather different effect produced by the use of the anaphoric 'and', see the summary of Criseyde's reply to Diomede's first expression of love as they ride together towards her father's tent (V. 183–89). It reads like an embarrassed scramble through a recital of mechanical compliments until relief arrives with the end of the journey and the conclusion of the stanza: 'As seyde she, and from hire hors shalighte'.

20. See P. E. Beichner, *Medieval Studies,* XIV (1952), 151–53.

21. (I. 1000–1). For a similar use of *post* in a religious context, cf. *CT.* I. 214.

22. *Op. cit.,* p. 152.

23. Pandarus is also associated with Genius, but in a different way, by Alice B. Miskimin, *The Renaissance Chaucer* (New Haven and London, 1975), pp. 179–80, and by Donald W. Rowe, *'O Love, O Charite!': Contraries Harmonized in Chaucer's Troilus* (Carbondale, Ill.: Southern Illinois Univ. Press, 1976), p. 89. (On this study, see below, Note 43).

24. In one respect his function is more like that of the Genius in Gower's *Confessio Amantis* who, besides acting as confessor of Amans, is also priest of Venus. For a recent discussion of the complex problem of Genius's significance in Gower, see Denise N. Baker, 'The Priesthood of Genius: A Study of the Medieval Tradition', *Speculum,* LI (1976), 277–91. For further comments on the passage in *NPT,* as well as for two comparisons between this tale and *Tr & C,* Book IV, see I. Bishop, '*The Nun's Priest's Tale* and the Liberal Arts', *RES* XXX (1979), 257–69.

25. *A Preface to Chaucer* (Princeton, 1963), p. 479. One reader who evidently does is Ida Gordon, *The Double Sorrow of Troilus* (Oxford, 1970), p. 126.

26. When, at V. 1213, he genuinely experiences 'woode jalousie', the surprising thing is that he has not felt it much earlier.

27. I do not imply by this that opera and psychological drama are incompatible. Indeed, a revealing comparison could be made between this episode in *Troilus* and the love-duet in the second act of Wagner's *Tristan* which also exploits the conventions of the *tagelied* or *alba.* There is almost too much dogmatic psychology in the way in which Wagner asserts the superiority of the claims of the realm of 'Night' over those of 'Day'.

28. Cf. IV. 1432–33.

29. Cf. one of Reason's many definitions of love in *The Romaunt of the Rose,* 'A sikernesse all set in drede' (4706).

30. For Chaucer's notion of 'tragedye', see the gloss in *Boece* ii. Prosa 2 (Robinson, ed., p. 331); also *CT.* VII. 1991–98, 2761–66 – and the intervening *exempla* of *Mnk. T.* At *CT.* VII. 2771–73 and 2774–77 the Knight gives, in effect, definitions of 'tragedye' and 'comedye' respectively, though without using these terms. In general the term 'comedy' meant little more than the narrative of an ascent 'fro wo to wele' and was applied to works as diverse as the Latin counterparts to fabliaux and Dante's divine triptych. See Dante's (?) discussion of the terms in Epistle to Can Grande della

Scala. On 'tragedy', see further W. Farnham, *The Medieval Heritage of Elizabethan Tragedy* (Berkeley, 1936). On pp. 97—100, 140—41 and 143, he notes how some of the biographies in Boccaccio's *De Casibus Virorum Illustrium* combine the ascending movement of 'comedye' and the descending movement of 'tragedye' to produce an ultimate 'tragedy' whose structure is pyramidal. This appears to be the nearest parallel to the double turn in the plot of Chaucer's 'litel ... tragedye' (V. 1786).

For critical discussion of *Tr & C* and 'tragedye', see the controversial essay by D. W. Robertson, 'Chaucerian Tragedy', *ELH*, XIX (1952), 1—37, reprinted (along with several other articles mentioned in the present study) in R. J. Schoeck and J. Taylor (edd.), *Chaucer Criticism: Vol. 2: Troilus and Criseyde and the Minor Poems* (Notre Dame, Indiana, 1961), pp. 86 ff. The essay is also substantially reproduced in Robertson's *A Preface to Chaucer* (see above, Note 25). Also J. Lawlor, *Chaucer* (London, 1968), Chap. 3: *'Tragedye* and Tragedy'. For a somewhat more sophisticated account of the interrelations between 'tragedye' and 'comedye', see D. W. Rowe, *'O Love, O Charite!'* (see below, Note 43), pp. 140—41; and Monica E. McAlpine, *The Genre of Troilus and Criseyde* (Cornell Univ. Press, Ithaca and London, 1978). She attributes the phrase 'litel myn tragedye' (V. 1786) to the 'narrator' rather than to Chaucer the author; she sees the story of Troilus as a 'Boethian comedy' and that of Criseyde as a 'Boethian tragedy' (Chapters 5 and 6 respectively). Her study contains some interesting insights and *obiter dicta*, but her reading of the poem differs from mine in many fundamental respects. For her discussion of the role of the 'narrator', see below, Note 84. Also relevant is P. Ruggiers, 'Notes Towards a Theory of Tragedy in Chaucer', *CR*, VIII (1973), 89—99. On the broader question of the dramatic mode of *Tr & C* (including a discussion of Chaucer's possible knowledge of Roman drama), see J. Norton-Smith, *Geoffrey Chaucer* (London, 1974), 160—212.

31. On structure, see S. B. Meech, *Design in Chaucer's Troilus* (Syracuse, New York, 1959). For a somewhat barren, statistical analysis, see W. Provost, *The Structure of Chaucer's Troilus* (Copenhagen, 1974).

32. Alice B. Miskimin, *The Renaissance Chaucer* (New Haven and London, 1975), pp. 202—03.

33. *Pace* R. M. Jordan, *Chaucer and the Shape of Creation* (Cambridge, Mass., 1967), who is not the only recent critic to argue that Chaucer participates in the 'Gothic' imagination which depends for its effects upon significant juxtaposition of detail rather than organic development. I agree about the importance of juxtapostion, but do not share the assumption that Chaucer's works cannot display 'organic form' because the concept had not yet been 'invented' by Coleridge.

34. The definition of love by contraries and paradoxes, which Chaucer here expands into an allegorical episode, is a common-place of medieval literature. For example, it is exploited with exhaustive virtuosity in the Lady Reason's 'discripcioun' of love in the *Roman de la Rose* (4701 ff. of the ME translation), where we are treated to a catalogue of oxymoronic metaphors. The couplet

> Also a swete helle it is,
> And a soroufull paradys
> (4743—44)

could easily have been the germ out of which the whole allegorical episode in the *Parlement* developed. It is present in Troilus's song (based on Petrarch); especially I. 400—13.

35. E.g., W. C. Curry, *Chaucer and the Medieval Sciences* (2nd ed., London, 1960), pp. 260—61. Curry's view of the passage has been challenged, and the unequivocal seriousness of these lines has been aptly questioned, by Patricia M. Kean, *Chaucer and the Making of English Poetry* (London, 1972), Vol. I, pp. 139—41.

36. For the appropriate association of *forncast,* cf. *CT* VII. 3217: 'By heigh ymaginacioun forncast'.

37. Some notable exceptions are: A. C. Spearing, *Criticism and Medieval Poetry*

(London 1964), p.108; S. Wenzel, 'Chaucer's Troilus of Book IV', *PMLA*, LXXIX (1964), 542–47; and I. Gordon, *The Double Sorrow of Troilus* (Oxford, 1970).

38. See below, p. 87.

39. Root, and other scholars subsequently, believe, on the evidence of different versions of the poem in MSS, that this meditation (like the account in Book V of the heavenward flight of the hero's soul) was added by Chaucer in a revision of the poem. If that is so, its purpose may have been to bring out more explicitly the philosophical implications – in a poem dedicated to 'philosophical Strode' – of the episode of the averted tragedy.

Whatever one may think about the need for such a speculative passage at this point in the action, it must be admitted that Troilus's speech is, in itself, an infelicitous composition. It reads like versified philosophy that has not been transmuted into poetry. (Contrast Troilus's speech in Shakespeare's *Troilus and Cressida*, V. ii. 126–57, which represents so vividly the lover's emotional perplexity at the metaphysical questions of Unity and Identity.) The poetic nadir is reached in the *exemplum* at IV. 1023–43, about the *see* (bench), which reminds one of the table which features as the invariable 'stage property' in discussions of the theory of solipsism in old-fashioned text-books on epistemology. No amount of special pleading on the part of critics who regard *Tr & C.* as a 'philosophical' poem designed to 'kis the steppes' (cf. V. 1791) of 'Boece' will ever undermine Root's celebrated comment on IV. 1027 (*ed. cit.,* p. 519).

40. IV. 496–97, and see below, p. 78.

41. See below, p. 87.

42. See below, p. 56.

43. For discussion of a more metaphysical aspect of the poem's dialectical procedure, see P. Elbow, *Oppositions in Chaucer* (Middletown, Connecticut, 1975), 49–72. For a symbolic and cosmological interpretation of contraries in the poem, see D. W. Rowe, *'O Love, O Charite!': Contraries Harmonized in Chaucer's Troilus* (Carbondale, Ill.: Southern Illinois Univ. Press, 1976). Although I agree with many of Mr. Rowe's observations about 'contraries', I find his account of their 'harmonization' unconvincing. His symbolic interpretations of characters, action and structure are sometimes far-fetched. Occasionally, in order to extract a favoured *sententia,* he distorts the *sensus* of a passage. See, for example, his remarks (pp. 46, 83, 96) on the reference to Janus at II. 77. He thinks it appropriate that this two-faced deity should be invoked to guide Pandarus (an ambivalent character) on his first visit to Criseyde who is 'double' (unlike the true Troilus). But he does not observe that Chaucer here invokes Janus specifically as 'god of entre'. It cannot, of course, be 'proved' that there is no allusion 'in the poem' to the attribute of the god which Mr. Rowe seizes upon, but no critic can afford to ignore the poet's explicit reason for introducing the demi-god (on which see below, pp. 58 and 59).

44. I. 1065–71 – and see above, p. 38.

45. Cf. Robinson, ed., p. 818; for text and translation of this treatise, see above, Note 6.

46. It is a 'romanticised' version of the incident described by Pandaro in Canto II. But it may also have been influenced by the episode in Canto VII where Deiphoebus overhears Troilus's complaint – though there the lady's name is unwittingly betrayed.

47. See above, p. 41. On the meaning and etymology of *Danger,* see C. S. Lewis, *The Allegory of Love* (Oxford, 1936), 364–66. Also *ibid.,* pp. 177 ff. for discussion of relationship between *Tr & C* and *Roman de la Rose.*

48. See above, p. 47.

49. See I. Bishop, 'The Narrative Art of *The Pardoner's Tale',* *Medium Aevum,* XXXVI (1967), 15–24; especially p. 19. Reprinted in J. J. Anderson (ed.), *Chaucer: The Canterbury Tales: A Casebook* (London, 1974), 209–21.

50. And cf. her comment at II. 589 ff.

51. E. T. Donaldson, *Speaking of Chaucer* (London, 1970), p. 66.
52. II. 776 – cf. *PoF*, 3.
53. For other interpretations of this episode, see Sister M. C. Borthwick, *MLQ*, XXII (1961), 232–35; I. Gordon, *The Double Sorrow of Troilus* (Oxford, 1970), pp. 97 ff.
54. For a different account of the significance of this dream, see A. C. Spearing, *Criticism and Medieval Poetry* (London, 1964), 100–08. This book makes a more significant contribution than the same quthor's *Chaucer: Troilus and Criseyde* (London, 1976), which is an elementary introduction to the poem.
55. According to medieval *Artes Dictaminis*, the *exordium* of an epistle is divided into the *salutatio* and the *captatio benevolentiae* (where 'humility formulas' properly occur). See J. J. Murphy (ed.), *Three Medieval Rhetorical Arts* (Berkeley, Los Angeles, London, 1971), xvi. He translates the complete text of a twelfth-century *Ars*, pp. 1–25. On Troilus's letter at V. 1317–1421 (not discussed here), see N. Davis in *RES* (NS), XVI (1965), 233–44.
56. See above, p. 54.
57. II. 1422–24. I take 'my frend', not as vocative, but as in apposition to 'Criseyde'.
58. Cf. *GGK* 917 and *CT*. V. 89–100.
59. On 'pronunciation' and gesture, see B. L. Joseph, *Elizabethan Acting* (London, 1951), who quotes this passage on p. 7.
60. See above, p. 67.
61. See above, p. 34.
62. *The Allegory of Love* (Oxford, 1936), p. 193.
63. *Ibid.*
64. A very pertinent comment on a different aspect of Pandarus's sensitivity on this occasion is made by B. L. Joseph, 'Troilus and Criseyde', *E & S* (1954), p. 53.
65. Cf. III. 71–80, and see above, p. 72.
66. This impression is increased when, in the temple scene, he again produces the same argument: 'Artow for hire and for noon other born?' (IV. 1095).
67. For the anchorite as 'dead' cf. *Ancrene Wisse* (*EETS* No. 249), pp. 30–31; 179.
68. Ida Gordon, *The Double Sorrow of Troilus*, p. 105, comments on the ineptitude of the allusion to Orpheus and Eurydice. For another reading of the whole episode, see D. W. Rowe, *'O Love, O Charite!'*, pp. 124–27.
69. See above, pp. 42; 49 ff.; 52.
70. Certainly, the narrator's self-defeating reassurances in IV. 1415–21 are an attempt to anticipate such a reaction.
71. See above, p. 60.
72. Cf. her 'anthology' of Pandarus's salient terms, discussed above, pp. 12, 54.
73. Boccaccio (*Il Filostrato*, IV) has the debate between Love and Reason, but he does not present it, as Chaucer does, in sharp counterpoint to the parliamentary debate.
74. For other accounts of the contention between Love and Reason in Book IV, see S. Wenzel, *PMLA*, LXXIX (1964), 542–47; I. Gordon, *The Double Sorrow of Troilus*, pp. 117 ff.
75. Only these first two lines of the stanza are translated from Boccaccio who, in any case, gives the whole speech to Troilo as an encomium of Criseida.
76. IV. 1566. See above, p. 86.
77. Cf. V. 1688 ff., for Troilus's bitter reaction to this particular concession.
78. *EETS* No. 249, p. 194. 'What do men and women suffer for false love and for unclean love? And how much more they would still be willing to suffer' (trans. M. Salu, *The Ancrene Riwle* [London, 1955], p. 168).
79. *Ibid.*, p. 201. I have silently expanded abbreviations, joined divided words and modernised punctuation. 'There is often great love between man and woman. But it might happen that a woman, even though she were married to one man, might grow

112

depraved and prostitute herself so long with others, that although she might wish to return to him, he would not want her. Christ, then, loves more than this, for even if His spouse, the soul, prostitutes herself with the fiend in mortal sin many a year and a day, His mercy is always waiting for her when she wants to leave the devil and come home again' (Salu, p. 174).

80. See above, p. 17.

81. See above, p. 87.

82. There is no counterpart in *Il Filostrato* to the italicised words, whereas the reference to the negative action of Fortune (V. 1763–64) is merely translated from Boccaccio. As for the parenthetic 'as god wolde' (IV. 1212): there is no equivalent at the corresponding point of *Il Filostrato*, but Criseida does later attribute their deliverance to providence.

83. It has been discussed most learnedly and extensively by J. M. Steadman, *Disembodied Laughter* (Berkeley, Los Angeles, London, 1972). Another discussion of the literary and philosophical background to this episode, and its sequel, will be found in P. M. Kean, *Chaucer and the Making of English Poetry* (London, 1972), Vol. I, pp. 159–74.

84. Much has been written about the distinction between Chaucer the author and the 'narrator of the poem', who is sometimes conceived of as a fictionalised figure with an identity and personality of his own. The most notable of such discussions is in E. T. Donaldson, *Speaking of Chaucer* (London, 1970), pp.65–83 (and see above, my Note 7); *ibid.*, pp. 84–101 (essay entitled 'The Ending of *Troilus*'). Also the same author's *Chaucer's Poetry: An Anthology for the Modern Reader* (New York, 1958), pp. 966–67, and ff. See also C. Muscatine, *Chaucer and the French Tradition* (Berkeley and Los Angeles, 1957), esp. pp. 135 ff. and 161–65; G. Shepherd in D. S. Brewer (ed.), *Chaucer and Chaucerians* (London, 1966), pp. 71 ff; J. Lawlor, *Chaucer* (London, 1968), pp.63–69; I. Gordon, *The Double Sorrow of Troilus* pp.61–92; D. W. Rowe, *'O Love, O Charite!',* Chapter 5, *passim.* For the latest discussion, see Monica E. McAlpine, *The Genre of Troilus and Criseyde* (Cornell Univ. Press, Ithaca and London, 1978), Chapter 4, *passim:* also pp. 35 ff. This part of her discussion is marred (p. 38) by an unfortunate misunderstanding of the verb *leigh* (II. 1077) – doubly unfortunate as the error is repeated on p. 154 where it materially affects her account of Troilus's development. (See also above, my Note 30).

For my own part, I regard the figure of the narrator principally as a device for manipulating the reader's or listener's responses to the action. I would not care to treat this narrator as a subject for psycho-analysis. Closely related to the question of the 'invented' narrator is that of the 'imagined' audience, on which see Dieter Mehl in B. Rowland (ed.), *Chaucer and Middle English Studies in Honour of Rossell Hope Robbins* (London, 1974), pp.173–89. Also relevant are the remarks on 'manuscript poetry' in D. S. Brewer's essay on *Tr & C* in W. F. Bolton (ed.), *The Middle Ages* (Vol. I of *Sphere History of Literature in the English Language* [1970]), pp. 195 ff.

85. Cf. Laȝamon's *Brut*, 1037; *St. Erkenwald*, 25.

86. *EETS* No. 249, p. 208. 'So exceedingly does He love love that He makes her His equal. I dare to say even more – He makes her His sovereign and does all she commands, as if from necessity.' (Salu, p. 180).

87. For the most perceptive study of Chaucer's notions of Venus, see J. A. W. Bennett, *The Parlement of Foules: An Interpretation* (Oxford, 1957), especially pp. 93 ff. and ch. III *passim.* See also D. S. Brewer (ed.), *The Parlement of Foulys* (London and Edinburgh, 1960). For a recent account of thirteenth- and fourteenth-century discussions of Venus, see E. G. Schreiber, 'Venus in Medieval Mythographic Tradition', *JEGP*, LXXIV (1975), 519–35. D. W. Rowe, *'O Love, O Charite!'* (pp. 92 ff.) finds the Prologue to Book III ambivalent in its conceptions of Love and Venus; but his conclusions differ from mine.

88. For a discussion of the relationship between Eros and Agape, see M. C. D'Arcy, *The Mind and Heart of Love* (London, 1945).

89. Cf. B. Smalley, *English Friars and Antiquity in the Early Fourteenth Century* (Oxford, 1960); J. B. Allen, *The Friar as Critic* (Nashville, 1971); also Schreiber, *art. cit.*

90. Cf. *LGW*, 1039—42; G. L. Brook (ed.), *The Harley Lyrics* (Manchester, 1948), p. 39 — conclusion of 'The Fair Maid of Ribblesdale'. Other examples noted by J. Bayley, *The Characters of Love* (London, 1960), p. 104 (in a chapter devoted to *Tr & C*).

91. See above, p. 45.

92. See above, p. 20.

93. On the interpretation of the *Parlement*, see Bennett, *op. cit.*, and Brewer, *ed. cit.*

94. On the metaphorical anatomy of the heart and mind in patristic and medieval authors, see E. R. Curtius, *European Literature and the Latin Middle Ages*, trans. W. R. Trask (London, 1953), pp. 136—38. The eyes of the heart are mentioned in *Ancrene Wisse*, Pt. VII — see ed. by G. Shepherd (London and Edinburgh, 1959), note to p. 19, line 26. Cf. also *Tr & C*, I. 453: 'His herte, which that is his brestes ye'.

95. *EETS* No. 249, pp. 204—05. ' "I would", He says to His beloved, "that in loving Me you were either utterly cold or utterly hot, but because you are as it were lukewarm, between the two, neither hot nor cold, you disgust Me, and unless you grow hotter, I will vomit you out." ' (Salu, p. 177).

SELECT BIBLIOGRAPHY

(N.B. This list is confined to editions and studies of *Troilus and Criseyde* that are cited elsewhere in the present volume.)

A. EDITIONS

R. K. ROOT (ed.), *The Book of Troilus and Criseyde* (Princeton, 1926).

F. N. ROBINSON (ed.), *The Works of Geoffrey Chaucer* (2nd ed., London, 1957).

R. K. GORDON, *The Story of Troilus* (New York, 1964). [Contains a text of *Tr & C* and of Henryson's *Testament of Cressid,* together with prose translation of Boccaccio's *Il Filostrato* and excerpts from Benoît de Sainte-Maure.]

B. MONOGRAPHS ON TROILUS AND CRISEYDE

IDA GORDON, *The Double Sorrow of Troilus* (Oxford, 1970).

MONICA E. McALPINE, *The Genre of Troilus and Criseyde* (Cornell Univ. Press, Ithaca and London, 1978).

S. B. MEECH, *Design in Chaucer's Troilus* (Syracuse, New York, 1959).

W. PROVOST, *The Structure of Chaucer's Troilus* (Copenhagen, 1974).

D. W. ROWE, *'O Love, O Charite!': Contraries Harmonized in Chaucer's Troilus* (Carbondale, Ill.: Southern Illinois Univ. Press, 1976).

A. C. SPEARING, *Chaucer: Troilus and Criseyde* (London, 1976).

J. M. STEADMAN, *Disembodied Laughter* (Berkeley, Los Angeles, London, 1972).

C. COLLECTIONS OF ESSAYS ON TROILUS AND CRISEYDE

MARY SALU (ed.), *Essays on Troilus and Criseyde* (Cambridge, 1979). [I have been unable to make use of this work, as it had not appeared before the present volume went to press.]

R. J. SCHOECK and J. TAYLOR (edd.), *Chaucer Criticism:* Vol. 2: *Troilus and Criseyde and the Minor Poems* (Notre Dame, Indiana, 1961). [Contains the articles by Lewis and Robertson mentioned below.]

D. GENERAL WORKS (MOSTLY ON CHAUCER) THAT INCLUDE SUBSTANTIAL DISCUSSIONS OF TROILUS AND CRISEYDE

BAYLEY, *The Characters of Love* (London, 1960).

. CURRY, *Chaucer and the Medieval Sciences* (2nd ed., London, 1960).

DONALDSON, *Chaucer's Poetry: An Anthology for the Modern Reader* (New York, 1958).

peaking of Chaucer (London, 1970).

OW, *Oppositions in Chaucer* (Middletown, Connecticut, 1975).

THY EVERETT, *Essays on Middle English Literature* (Oxford, 1955).

ORDAN, *Chaucer and the Shape of Creation* (Cambridge, Mass., 1967).

A M. KEAN, *Chaucer and the Making of English Poetry,* Vol. I (London,).

R, *Chaucer* (London, 1968).

, *The Allegory of Love* (Oxford, 1936).

ISKIMIN, *The Renaissance Chaucer* (New Haven and London, 1975).

C. MUSCATINE, *Chaucer and the French Tradition* (Berkeley and Los Angeles, 1957).

J. NORTON-SMITH, *Geoffrey Chaucer* (London, 1974).

D. W. ROBERTSON, *A Preface to Chaucer* (Princeton, 1963).

A. C. SPEARING, *Criticism and Medieval Poetry* (London, 1964).

J. SPEIRS, *Chaucer the Maker* (London, 1951).

E. ARTICLES ON TROILUS AND CRISEYDE

SISTER M. C. BORTHWICK, 'Antigone's Song as "Mirour" in Chaucer's *Troilus and Criseyde', MLQ,* XXII (1961), 232—35.

D. S. BREWER, '*Troilus and Criseyde*', in W. F. Bolton (ed.), *The Middle Ages* (Vol. I of *Sphere History of Literature in the English Language* [London, 1970], pp. 195—228).

N. DAVIS, 'The *Litera Troili* and English Letters', *RES* (NS), XVI (1965) 233—44.

T. B. HANSON, 'Criseyde's Brows Once Again', *N & Q,* CCXVI (1971), 285—86.

B. L. JOSEPH, '*Troilus and Criseyde*', *E & S,* Vol. 7 of New Series (1954), 42—61.

C. S. LEWIS, 'What Chaucer Really Did to *Il Filostrato',* *E & S,* XVII (1932 56—75.

D. MEHL, 'The Audience of *Troilus and Criseyde',* in B. Rowland (ed.), *Chaucer an Middle English Studies in Honour of Rossell Hope Robbins* (London, 1974 pp. 173—89.

R. A. PRATT, 'Chaucer and *Le Roman de Troyle et de Criseida*', *SP,* LIII (1956) 609—39.

D. W. ROBERTSON, 'Chaucerian Tragedy', *ELH,* XIX (1952), 1—37.

P. RUGGIERS, 'Notes Towards a Theory of Tragedy in Chaucer', *CR,* VIII (1973 89—99.

ELIZABETH SALTER, '*Troilus and Criseyde:* A Reconsideration', in J. Lawlor (ed. *Patterns of Love and Courtesy* (London, 1966), pp. 86—106.

G. SHEPHERD, '*Troilus and Criseyde*', in D. S. Brewer (ed.), *Chaucer an Chaucerians* (London, 1966), pp. 65—87.

S. WENZEL, 'Chaucer's Troilus of Book IV', *PMLA,* LXXIX (1964), 542—47.